SUCCESS IS MY PREY

PREY

LESSONS THAT WILL HELP YOU
ELEVATE IN LIFE

BY
Jared "J.ANDERS" Smith

DISCLAIMER

The advice contained in this material might not be suitable for everyone. The author designed the information to present his opinion about the subject matter. The reader must carefully investigate all aspects of any business decision before committing him or herself. The author obtained the information contained herein form sources he believes to be reliable and from his own personal experience, but he neither implies nor intends any guarantee of accuracy. The author is not in the business of giving legal, accounting, or any other type of professional advice. Should the reader need such advice, he or she must seek services from a competent professional. The author particularly disclaims any liability, loss, or risk taken by individuals who directly or indirectly act on the information contained herein. The author believes the advice presented here is sound, but readers cannot hold him responsible for either the actions they take or the risk taken by individuals who directly or indirectly act on the information contained herein.

Published by A&K Publishing, LLC

A division of J.ANDERS Enterprises, LLC

Printed in the United States

Design by Hubspot Pro

Copyright © 2020 by Jared Smith

ISBN 978-1-7349804-0-0

Dedication

This book is dedicated to my wonderful wife Ashley Smith, and our beautiful daughters, Ashyra and Kamirah Smith. It is because of them why I do what I do today.

I would also like to dedicate this book to my mother Ellisha Davis, and my father Jared Smith Sr. I love you both.

I would also like to dedicate this book to my extended family and friends who have been by my side and supporting me throughout my journey in life.

Finally, I would like to dedicate this book to the millions around the world who seek to take their life to higher levels.

I have a burning desire to be the voice of the Underdog. I seek to inspire and motivate anyone who had to start out with the odds stacked against them. My definite purpose is to show people that no matter where you come from or your circumstances, you can do and have anything you put your mind to. I achieve this outcome by living my truth and using my truth as an example for others. I strive to provide the best possible book that will help and empower anyone who reads it!

- MR. J. ANDERS

TABLE OF CONTENTS

The Beginning of the Previews

If you were to ask anyone who knows me personally, they will tell you that I can talk your ear off. In fact, some will probably tell you that I annoy them when I start talking. However, if you also ask anyone who knows me personally, they will tell you that I have a very high and positive energy drive. Anyone who knows me personally, will most likely tell you that I am a very motivational guy. To be honest, you can probably just see it for yourself if you follow me on social media.

This high energetic, motivational, and ambitious spirit that drives me today is because of two things: I wanted my future to be better than my past, and I knew I was born to be great. One common thing that I have heard from family, friends, and even strangers that I've talked to over the years is that I should be a motivational speaker. To be honest, when I began hearing that statement, I didn't give it much thought. I just knew that I've always loved to help others. I have always genuinely wanted to see others win in life, but I've never actually thought about becoming a speaker or helping others on a large scale until after years of hearing those statements from peers around me. One reason I didn't take the whole motivational speaking thing serious is because I grew up with a speech impediment. I stuttered over my words a lot. Between the ages of four through six, I had to stomp my feet, just to get my words out. I used to be like a CD that skips in the CD player because it's so scratched up. As I was growing up over the years, I was afraid to approach girls because of my stuttering issue. I hated reading out loud or giving presentations in classes. I used to feel extremely embarrassed about my speech. So this reason alone made me fearful of public speaking.

However, as I became older, I outgrew the bad stuttering in my speech, and my confidence started to really grow. It's still there a little bit, but not as severe as stomping my feet or taking five minutes just to get out one word. If I stutter a little now, it's probably because I'm talking too fast and get tongue twisted.

Today, I am a trained professional with a motivational speaking certificate from the International Association of Professions Career College. I also joined a local chapter with Toastmasters International, where I aimed to improve my communication skills and build my leadership skills. I have received direct training from world renowned speaker Brian Tracy. Those organizations, along with Mr. Tracy, have really helped me build the necessary skills, build my confidence, and remove my fear of speaking publicly.

The more fearless I became about talking, the more I talked; the more I talked, the more I connected with people; the more I connected with people, the more I enjoyed serving people; the more fascinated I became with serving people, the less I feared about motivational speaking.

This book almost didn't happen...

Even after support from peers, receiving training, and removing my fear of talking, I was still hesitant on actually getting started. I started having doubts and questioning whether people would actually like me or not. What would I speak about? Why would anyone want to listen to me in the first place? What can I teach others as a young person?

I had one person who told me not to try motivational speaking or even write a book, because I hadn't "accomplished enough" yet. The funny part is that this individual is a family member!

So, because I actually listened to that individual, I contemplated for the longest about speaking and writing this book. I would start writing then stop, and then I would start and stop again. This was an on and off cycle. I thought that maybe since I hadn't yet reached the "pinnacle" of my success, I wasn't qualified to speak or write. I thought I needed to be "well known" in order for me to write my first book. I thought I had to be 40 years old with lots of life experiences under my belt in order for me to write my first book. So I put off writing the book for a while and started my first company, THE J.ANDERS BRAND™ which is a clothing brand.

Over time while I was working on building my brand, I kept thinking about speaking and releasing a book. I kept thinking about the messages that were within me. The more I talked to people, the more confirmation I was receiving about speaking and writing this book to help someone. The more I shared my thoughts on social media, the more I felt compelled to write this book.

The realization that occurred to me is that I didn't need validation from anyone else when it comes to my life. I feel like I am "successful" in my own right. I don't need a multi-million dollar company established or need to be a well-known public figure in order to share my story and help someone. I think we can all learn from one another no matter what age we are. I think kids can teach an adult, just as adults can teach children.

With that being said, I urge you to dive into this book with an open mind and be encouraged to learn. You may know some of the information in this book, or it may be totally new information to you. Either way, I hope that sharing these thoughts or principles that I've learned throughout my life will help and impact you positively in your own life.

Success to you may mean something different to me, but that's not the point here. My goal with this book is to help you elevate in life. You will hear my pain and failures as well as my happiness and success. This will be a great book for you to not only gain inspiration from, but also to pass along and share with others. So, get ready to read, learn, and elevate! LETS GOOOOOOO!

Chapter 1

Overcoming Generational Curses

"It's not how you are born...it's how you die."

Like me, you may have grown up with the odds stacked against you from the beginning. Looking back at my family's history and the environment that I was born into, it seems like the word "success" was foreign in the country towns of Union and Kelton, South Carolina, which is where I was born and spent some of my early childhood years.

I come from a family of felons, because getting in trouble, fighting, drinking, etc. is really all that they knew growing up. The memories that come to mind when I think about Union and Kelton, is witnessing family getting drunk, fighting, dropping out of school, and going to jail. I've watched people that I love do dope right in front of me. I've actually seen a crack rock (I've never done crack myself). I saw family sit around and drink Olde English 800. They used to even ask me to bring them a beer or throw away their cigarettes for them. I've watched my uncles fight one another, and my mother fight one of my uncles multiple times, including one time while she was pregnant with my younger brother.

Everyone on my maternal side of the family has been to jail; from my grandparents and on down. I remember going to visit family members whenever they went to jail. I remember going to visit my dad in Indiana, when he was serving a small federal sentence in a penitentiary. Seeing this reality in my family made me wonder if I was really supposed to be "successful."

Visiting my dad in the pen wasn't nearly as painful as seeing my mom go away, but I'll get into that later. The first time that I actually felt like I experienced pain in my life was when I witnessed my mother getting arrested right before my eyes and ultimately get sentenced to prison. The police pulled up outside and knocked on the door. She quickly ran into the back room and got under the bed. She called me back there and told me to tell them that she wasn't there. Before I could get back to the hallway, the police had burst through the trailer looking for her, and of course, it didn't take long for them to find her.

For the next six months, during my first grade year of school, I had to visit my mom at a prison in Columbia, South Carolina. I'll never forget how I used to daydream about her every day in class. I had lost all motivation for school. My grades were awful because of her absence. I felt like I had lost everything in life, and I was only in the first grade. Call me a mama's boy or whatever, but there's no love like a mother's love in this world.

I'll never forget the day when she was released, and she was at home waiting on me and my sister to get off the school bus. Boy, the joy in my heart! We ran to her as she ran to us, and it was a moment that I will never forget. After I was back reunited with my mother, my grades went right back up, and I finished my first grade year off strong.

Georgia Bound

The summer between first and second grade, my maternal grandma was transferring to Georgia with her job. My mom decided to join my grandma and move us to Georgia as well. She was determined to better her life and put me and my sister in a better environment. She was determined not to raise us in Union and Kelton because she refused to have us grow up the way that she had to.

When we arrived in Georgia, my mom set goals for herself that she wanted to achieve. Already a single mother with two children and pregnant with a third, at the age 25, she enrolled into an adult education program and set a goal to obtain her GED. After receiving her GED, she then went on to put herself through college twice: one degree in cosmetology, and one in pediatrics (cosmetology has always been her true passion; she owns her own hair salon business today!).

Like most single mothers, my mom had to rely on government assistance, such as Section 8 and food stamps. So, as you can probably imagine, I grew up in the "projects" or "the hood" as we say. 363 Crest Circle in Lavonia, Georgia was the first Section 8 housing we lived in. Lavonia became our second home.

Second grade school year started off interesting. The elementary school that I was attending, Lavonia Elementary, had placed me in special education classes, because they thought I was a slow learner and needed special attention. I think partly because of my grades from the year prior, but I think partly because I had that stuttering problem.

So, I went to the special education classes, and the funny thing is, I actually loved it. The work was super-duper easy; we baked brownies, rice krispy treats, and things like that. Despite all the fun I was having, and how much I loved special ed, I was only in there for two weeks until they moved me back to a regular class. They told me that I was excelling very well, and they did not see a reason for me to be in there. I went on throughout elementary school being on both the honor roll and principle's list, every time report cards came out.

Things were definitely looking up for my mom after the move to Georgia. Yes, we were living in the projects, but it wasn't anything like Kelton, where I had grown up. One thing about growing up in the Crest Circle projects and the Lavonia community is that it felt like a true family culture. We had our own little basketball league that the older guys had put together to keep us young kids active and out of trouble. We had our own neighborhood snack lady who sold snacks and drinks to the kids for twenty-five cents while we would be outside playing (every real hood had a snack lady). We had big neighborhood cookouts. We had track meets around the block. We had monopoly and bingo family game nights. We played kickball. We raced on bikes. We even had an afterschool program that was put in place by a lady named Mrs. Sheena to help us with our school work in the afternoons.

Kids from the other projects named Goose Holla would come over to ours, and we would go over to theirs. We didn't have any family in Georgia, but Crest Circle, Goose Holla, and the Lavonia community became our family.

While I may reminisce on the good times we had in the projects, I'm also reminded of the not so good side. I don't think I could go back and live in the projects again. When we moved to the Wood Street projects in Toccoa, GA, I started seeing drug dealing, drug busts, dope fiends, shootouts, more fights, etc. We were so immune to the gunshots that we stopped getting scared whenever we heard them. The childhood fun in the projects definitely grew old as I was getting into my teenage years. I knew there was a better life, and I wanted that better life.

I think everyone has the opportunity to make it out of that environment, but not everyone takes the opportunity to get out. One problem with most people in the hood is that they take the government assistance and get too comfortable. You can't live on government assistance and make good money in this world, otherwise you wouldn't need the assistance. You're limited as to how much money you can make (legally) before you're considered ineligible for government assistance. Therefore, many people settle for the low paying jobs and live in the projects for decades.

Not only were there financial limitations when living in the projects, there were also mental limitations. Many of us weren't thinking about "success," let alone striving for it. We weren't thinking about success because we didn't see success around us. We weren't having conversations about success, because we weren't around many people who had built success for themselves. Instead, our minds were set on simply surviving and making it to the next day. We weren't being taught how to build our future.

We would often envy the middle-class kids because we felt that they had a better life than we had. While we were engaging in things like video games, they were reading books. While we were focused on clothes and shoes, they were being taught how to manage money and build credit. While we were looking at our poor class reality, every day, they were traveling and seeing new places. They had stories about how nice their vacations were, and we were having stories about a recent shootout or who had just went to jail.

I'm not trying to bash anyone here by no means, because my parents didn't know what they didn't know, and your parents didn't know what they didn't know. They did their best with what they did know, and what they had to work with. And if you had parents like my mother, then your parents probably told you that they wanted you to be better than them. Pick up where they left off but elevate it; take it to another level for your children.

I gave you a brief background of my family to show that no one in my family, in the generations before, left a positive blueprint behind for the young folks like myself to follow. I only saw what NOT to do, but no examples of what TO do.

Every single person in my immediate family has been to jail. Yes, they went to jail because they committed crimes, but if you dig a little deeper, I'd say they went to jail because of their physical, mental, and financial conditions during those time periods. Those were the very same conditions that I had to grow up in as well.

Sidenote: THEY ARE ALL DOING GREAT TODAY, AND HAS ELEVATED FROM THEIR PAST CIRCUMSTANCES! I'M EXTREMELY PROUD OF THEM AND WHERE THEY ARE TODAY!

I remember back in 2009 when I was 17 in Atlanta. Rapper Gucci Mane released the song called "Wasted." The chorus started like, *"rock star lifestyle might don't make it/ living life high every day click wasted/ sipping on purple stuff rolling up the stanky."* That song had a major influence on me in 2009, because I was literally living life wasted that year. I was smoking after school every day with the boys, getting sloppy drunk at all of the parties, I was making fast money, and it wasn't a female that I couldn't have.

The point is that the song was telling me everything to do to get wasted, and how to successfully waste my life, and I was doing just that. I found myself living the exact lifestyle that I had watched my older family members consume when I was a young boy. That wasted lifestyle led to me catching a felony charge, facing a maximum of 20 years. Now I have been added to the list of family members who have been to jail and have caught felonies (we'll discuss that experience more in next chapter). And so, the curse continues.

See The Change, Be The Change

Take a look at your family's history. What bad habits or curses do you notice that have been taking place throughout your family? Look at how you can take things to another level in your family. Whether you have children, choose to have children someday or not, or have nieces or nephews, I urge

you not to let another generation be wasted. Be the generation that sees the change and become that change. I believe in generational curses, and I believe they can certainly be broken. I'm almost always engaging in conversations with older people because I love to hear their stories and learn from them. If you pay attention to the older generation, you will hear many of them talk about the things that they regret not doing when they were my age or your age. Many of them will say things like, "If I was your age, I would do this differently,"
or "I wish I could go back and do it all over again."

Many of them were just playing the hand that they were dealt. They couldn't help the situations that they were born into, just like you and I couldn't change what we were born into. But it's not how we are born into this world; it's about what we do during out lifetime and how we leave this world. In other words, it's not how you start, it's how you finish.

> **If you are older and reading this book, let me remind you that it is not too late for you. The past is a place of reference, not a place of residence. Move forward and stop living in regret. You can still help set up the younger generation from where you are today. You might not have had the tools when you were younger, and you probably wasted time, but it's never too late to start right now. **

In order to take ourselves and our families to higher levels, we must refrain from negative thoughts and actions, and seek to turn generational curses into positive generational trends. Become the trailblazer in your family. We have to feed our minds with positive affirmations daily, and recondition the way that we think about our lives if we truly want to elevate. What kind of example will you set for the next generation? Do you want to continue to pass down generational curses, or pass along positive generational habits?

#SuccessIsMyPreyChallenge: Challenge yourself to be the change you want to see.

Chapter 2

Embrace Your Past

"To have once been a criminal is no disgrace. To remain a criminal is the disgrace."- Malcolm X

"Askin' God to cleanse my pain and turn my pain into passion/ forgave myself for past mistakes, I'm not afraid to look backwards/- Rap artist, Kevin Gates

No one likes to discuss their past, but in my opinion, in order to live a peaceful and successful life, you must be at peace with your past. Therefore, you must face your past, regardless of how painful it may be; but ONLY use your past as a reference; not to reside there. We must refer back to the past to learn from lessons and mistakes, and to use it as motivation. I'm pretty transparent about mine, and I'm not ashamed, because I know it has helped me become who I am today.

I opened the first chapter discussing my family's history and overcoming generational curses. I'll go a little bit deeper in this chapter and explain how my past filled me with the ambition and drive that I have today, and how you can learn from it.

I mentioned the year 2009 in the first chapter and how that lifestyle drove me to a felony charge, facing a maximum of 20 years, so I'll start off by saying the year 2009 was an eventful year for me. It was the year that we moved out of the "hood" and left Section 8 housing when my mom attempted to buy her first house. The house attempt failed, and we landed ourselves in Norcross, GA, off of Jimmy Carter Boulevard (North Atlanta. The NAWF as we called it. You may have heard the rap group Migos mention it).

While the home purchase was in process, we lived in an Extended Stay hotel, just off of the boulevard that whole summer. There was a QuikTrip gas station right in front of the hotel, and this was the summer when I first fell in love with the QuikTrip gas station. I had met my friend Davion (R.I.P) who lived at the same hotel, and we along with a few others used to climb into the QuikTrip dumpster every night and eat those fresh foods and pastries that they had just thrown away. The food itself never touched the dumpster because it was in a plastic bag. We were hungry, and found a way to feed ourselves at night. Also, someone (I still don't know who) used to order Chick-fil-A catering and serve us chicken sandwiches every Tuesday.

Speaking of Davion, he became my right-hand man that summer. We had a lot in common. Being the oldest amongst our siblings, we were trying to find ways to take the pressure away from our mothers. We walked up and down Jimmy

Carter Boulevard almost every day, because we were bored and tired of being in our hotel rooms all day. We played a lot of pick-up basketball at Best Friend Park. That's where I won a pair of shoes from an older guy after walking around with the same pair of shoes with holes every day. And since the area was a heavy drug dealing area, we would often go to drug dealers' rooms, and we smoked weed and rolled dice with them.

We never really had any money, but whenever we had a few dollars, we would take some gambles and win money from others. We had our girlfriends who also lived at the same hotel, and we would often double-date and go to the $2 movies. We would even go to the mall and steal clothes together. We were some broke teenagers that summer and was just trying to survive by any means.

After months of living in that hotel and the house purchase being unsuccessful, my mother finally found us an apartment complex to move to, on the other end of Jimmy Carter Boulevard. Like everywhere we had moved, I quickly made some friends in that neighborhood. The crew that I started hanging with was definitely no good for me, but I couldn't see that at the time. We called ourselves GYG, which stood for "Guard Your Grill." You may or may not know, but Gwinnett County was the number one county in the state of Georgia for gang violence around that time, and GYG contributed to that because we were definitely heavy in those Gwinnett streets.

We all attended Meadowcreek High School (which is nicknamed "Ghettocreek"). You can imagine, just by the nickname of the school that we were up to no good as a school. I went to school with pretty much all the main gangs, and trust me, those guys were not playing about the gangs they were a part of. Shootouts in the area were the norm.

Every day after school, my crew and I had a routine. We would get off the school bus, smoke some blunts, go play basketball at the Lucky Shoals recreation center, and hang with some females. When the weekends came, we would go to a club in the city, someone's house party, or throw our own house party at one of our friend's apartment, whenever her mom wasn't home. Needless to say, we were living a young, wild, and free lifestyle.

We added one more thing into the mix, and this is when we really started getting more involved in the streets. We started "hitting licks," or the legal term, robbing. We started robbing people to try and put money in our pockets so we could maintain our already wild lifestyle, but for me, it started becoming bigger than that when I realized how much money I was making. The reason that I say it started becoming bigger for me is because I was determined to help my mom as much as possible.

The lifestyle that I was living was an outlet for my pain and anger, and the same is probably true for the rest of the guys that were in my crew. We lacked direction in our lives big time (just as the older generation had lacked direction in their youth also). None of our dads were active in our lives, so we didn't have a father figure to guide us as to how to be a man in this world. After applying for jobs around the area, and even being scammed out of jobs in downtown Atlanta, I started amplifying my robberies. I was doing more licks on my own. It was good, fast money.

Yes, what I was doing was wrong, but at the time, I just wanted to help my mom financially to take some pressure off of her, so I couldn't see the wrong that I was doing. My mom had four children to raise, and I felt that if I could just take care of myself and help my siblings, then that would take some worry and stress away from her. Seeing my mom hurt and hearing her cry in the room at night really hurt me. She didn't even know I could hear her crying.

Seeing eviction notices on the door, boiling water on the stove just to take a bath because the water was turned off, lighting the house with candles because the lights were turned off, heating the house with the stove open because we had no heat, and knowing your mom is doing the best that she could was a painful experience. When rapper Rodwave said, "Death gotta be easy, because life is hard," I truly felt that, because I literally was battling deep depression during those hard times.

There was a day, however, that I finally stopped the robberies, but it wasn't because I stopped on my own. I was forced to stop. It was my very first run in with the law. I remember the day like it was just yesterday.

It was Friday night November 6th, 2009. I went out to hit another lick that night, but I brought the crew along for this one. We did our normal routine. We all put on our ski masks, attended to our roles, did the robbery, and went back to our stash house. Normally, we would stash everything at our stash house, and then smoke while we waited a few hours before going home, just in case the police got a call about us and were searching for us.

So after we did our normal routine that night and began to walk home, we noticed there was a patrol car riding around our neighborhood. We kept walking normal, but we quickly started to sense that someone must have called GCPD (Gwinnett County Police Department). We were used to GCPD patrolling our neighborhood because of the crime in the area. Then we saw extra cars, and that's when we pretty much knew they had received a call about us and they were looking for us.

We took a few shortcuts through the neighborhood and got about two minutes from our apartments as one patrol car approached us. He quickly turned on his blue lights and put his alley light directly on us. Before we could take off running, five more cars pulled up, including two K-9 units, and they put those dogs on the ground so quick. I have outrun a lot of dogs in my young life, but I wasn't about to try those trained police dogs. I wasn't about to get eaten up by those German Shepherds.

I almost got myself shot by the police that night. When the police held us up at gunpoint and told us to show our hands, I wouldn't quite listen at first. I left my handgun at the stash house, but I forgot to leave my brass knuckles. I turned and threw them as far as I could, so I wouldn't get a charge for the brass knuckles. I was also very high, so I wasn't actually taking the process as serious as I should have been. But the last time I dropped my hands is when the officer got my full attention. The officer said, "If you drop your hands one more time, I will shoot you right where you are!" You better believe I threw my hands back up so fast and kept them up until they came and cuffed me. How many times have we seen young black males get shot by the police in this country?

As they were cuffing me, I watched my mom pull up in front of our apartment as she was just coming home from work. I knew that all she saw was some more blue lights in our neighborhood like any other night, but what she didn't know that it was her son getting arrested. They cuffed us and put us on the ground and searched us. They really started acting wild when they found bandanas in our pockets. They started calling us crazy names, and even kicked us a few times.

After all those crazy shenanigans, they put us in separate cars, and there I was in the back seat of a police car for the first time in my life, staring at my apartment. I tried to hold it together, but the tears started slowly coming down my face, because I knew that my mom was already doing the best that she could. I knew that receiving a call from her son in jail was going to hurt her more than anything. She didn't know what I was out there doing in those streets. As a matter of fact, none of my family knew. I had basketball workouts the next morning, but that got canceled because I was now on my way to the police station to be interrogated.

Because I had just turned 17 just a month before, I was going to be charged and tried as an adult for Strong Armed Robbery, a charge that carries a maximum sentence of 20 years. One of the other guys was charged as a juvenile, and the other guys never got charged. So, it was no co-defendants, and no going to juvenile for me. I was going straight to the big county jail. And so, my case begins....

The State of Georgia Vs Jared Smith Jr

In jail they placed me on the floor and in a pod with all of the high crime people. I was in there with capital murderers, rapists, and other high-profile criminals. I didn't have a bond, so I wasn't just about to get right back out like I hoped I would.

Due to this being my very first run-in with the law, and my lack of understanding the system, I had a public defender lawyer as my first lawyer. I found out very quickly why having a public defender is not good. I went for my first bond hearing on December 10th, 2009, and not knowing what I was signing at the time, the lawyer had me sign a waiver agreeing to waive my bond hearing. Because I waived my bond hearing, I couldn't be heard that day by the judge to set me a possible bond, so I had to sit in jail a little while longer. Let me remind you that I was still in high school during this time.

My mama and family helped get a private lawyer, and when I went back for another bond hearing on January 14th, 2010, I got granted a bond. My judge at the time, Mrs. Debra K. Turner, really made a tremendous impact on me. On the day she set my bond, she told me, "Young man, do you realize that you're facing up to a maximum of 20 years for this charge?" I'd never felt so many knots in my stomach.

It was like I literally became weak and sick in that very moment when I heard that. So in sudden shock, I replied, "Yes ma'am." Then she went on to say, "Young man, I don't normally set bonds for these types of charges in my court, but I have a good spirit about you, so I'm going to set you a bond at $25,000 with the conditions of you being on house arrest until your case is over. If you get into any trouble during the process of your case, then you will be brought back with no bond and sit here until your case is resolved. Do you understand that?" I heard her loud and clear, and on January 17th, 2010, I bonded out and had an ankle monitor on my leg for the next eight months.

While I was in there, I learned how to play chess, and with the chance that the judge took on me, I knew that being back out on the streets was also a chess game. I knew one wrong move could cost me, and I was determined to not let them get the upper hand. The house arrest was $75 a week that my mom had to pay in order to keep me from returning to jail, so that was a battle within itself, seeing that my mom was already struggling with other bills.

While I was on house arrest, I was only allowed to go to school and church, but returning back to Meadowcreek High wasn't so easy. Because I was inactive at school for an extended period of time, they told me that the only way I could get back into the Gwinnett County School System was to go to an alternative school. Unfortunately, I couldn't even get into the alternative school either, so like other family members, I became a dropout as well. Once I found out that I couldn't attend school anymore, I turned to my last option: get my GED.

I signed up for the GED program at Gwinnett Technical College and started the road to obtaining my GED. After a few months went by, my family and I had to quickly move to Douglasville (just past Six Flags) because the bills were getting more and more expensive for my mom in Gwinnett, and one of those bills was indeed that weekly ankle monitor payment. So, I had to put my GED on pause.

I was trying to remain as strong as I could, but seeing my mother struggle and to know that I was more of a burden on her with this ankle monitor on my leg just pained me more than anything. During this time, I battled with lots of mental health issues that no one knew about. I battled with depression big time. I was battling with thoughts to get back into the streets to make some money versus my desire to stay strong. My mind was in a crossroads, and I was trying my best to hold it together.

On June 27th, 2010, it got even tougher for my family and me. I was watching the BET Awards show that night and texting my girlfriend Coya at the time, when I received a phone call from the bonding company that was monitoring my ankle monitor. They told me that my ankle monitor was going dead and that it needed charging, but I had recently taken the monitor off the charger, so I thought that was kind of a strange phone call.

A few moments later came a knock on the front door. My sister opened the door, and before I knew it, two bounty hunters came storming into our trailer arresting me. The phone call that I received from the bonding company was a setup call to make sure that I was actually at home so that they could arrest me. I went back to Gwinnett County jail that night due to being about five weeks behind on the house arrest payments. My mom tried the best she could, but the payments were just unbearable. This time, my mom and younger siblings, my family, had to watch me get arrested and put into the back of a black Tahoe to return to jail.

Before heading back to Gwinnett County, the bounty hunters had to go to Kennesaw, GA to catch another guy who was also on house arrest. During the ride, all I could think about was how long I was going to have to sit in that jail until my case was resolved, just as the judge had told me. The bounty hunters located the apartment that they were looking for and got occupied with trying to trap him like they did me.

While I was in the backseat with the handcuffs on, I discovered that the handcuffs were loose. They were loose enough for me to get out of them, make a break for it while the hunters were occupied, and call my mom once I made it somewhere safe, but once again, I felt like this was another test. I had a clear shot to run and get free. I knew I could have outrun those guys, and they would have never caught me. It was like one half of my mind was saying run, but the other half was saying stay put. I ended up listening to the better half and stayed put. I knew that fleeing would have made my situation worse. I just had to *trust the process* and keep faith that everything would work out.

Going to jail this time wasn't as shocking as the first time because I was familiar with how the process worked. I was concerned about how long I was going to have to sit in there, but I was also concerned about Coya. I knew I had to answer to her and her family because they knew nothing about what I was going through. I always had pants on around her and made sure that her leg or foot never hit my ankle monitor. I even got into the pool with her with pants on.

I didn't tell Coya about it because I didn't want to scare her away by thinking that I was this horrible person, when I knew in my heart that I was a good genuine guy who just got lost on the wrong path. I was in love and was afraid of ruining that. Without them knowing it, she and her family really helped keep me strong during the time that we dated.

I called Coya for about two days and talked about it with her. At first, she seemed to be understanding of where I was coming from, and her family was even going to try to help get me back out. But then on that last day, she said she couldn't be with me anymore. Her mom said it was best that she didn't be with me, and to be honest, I couldn't blame her. I wouldn't blame any parent for protecting their children, especially their daughter. I wasn't upfront about everything, so it was hard for her to trust me when I hadn't been completely honest. It wasn't fair to her, and she deserved a better guy than me at the time. We were young, but she was young and was doing great with school and was headed somewhere in life. I completely understood that, and it was no hard feelings towards her or her family.

Although it was looking like my battle had gotten tougher, it actually had gotten better in disguise. I was back in there for two weeks, and this time, I didn't have to see the judge for another bond. I was able to sign myself out on a signature bond and walk out with no ankle monitor! I just had to make sure to make all of my court dates until my case was resolved. For a little while, I got to experience being a true free man again and lighten the burden off of my mom. So, from that moment forward, I was truly trying to focus on becoming a better person.

"*Don't ever think it can't happen to you.*"

In the fall of 2010 we faced, yet, another obstacle. We would always get eviction notices because we were always behind on rent. The eviction notice in August of that year was our last eviction notice. It was our last one because we had to pack our stuff and get out. Mama just didn't have the money to pay. She had done everything she could, but it became unbearable. We had to put our things in a storage building and go back to a hotel to live in until our next move.

The payments on the storage building were also too much for my mom to keep up with, so eventually, we lost the storage and everything in it. All of our achievements, school awards, furniture – everything – gone in a blink of an eye. Material things can be replaced, but it's the achievements and awards that I miss the most. All I have are stories for my children.

The only thing we had was our basket of clothes at the hotel room. Let me remind you that during this time, my three younger siblings were still in school. It was a scary time for my mom, because the last people that she wanted to find out about our living situation was the Department of Social Services. She did her best to hold us together by keeping her faith and not giving up; she definitely did that. My nickname in the family is Rock, but Mama is the true rock!

We were in the hotel for a few weeks, and that also became another financial burden for Mama to maintain. When she could no longer pay the weekly hotel fee, we had officially hit rock bottom. We had to vacate the hotel, and now Mama, her four kids, and my granny who was living with us at the time, were on the streets.

With only our basket of clothes, with no family in Georgia (because our home family were in South Carolina, and Mama was very reluctant to go back to South Carolina because of her past there), and with no other options left, Mama had to quickly find us a homeless shelter. We found a shelter in another area of Atlanta. My granny had to split from us and go to a separate shelter, but granny eventually made her way back to South Carolina to be with my aunt. Who would have ever thought that we'd be homeless and living in a shelter?

The thing about living in a shelter is that we had to leave the shelter at 6 a.m. in the morning and couldn't return until 6 p.m. that evening. If you didn't make it back before they locked the doors around 6 p.m., then you would not able to get in, and would have to sleep on the streets. That created another problem. The problem was that my mom would have to work during the daytime, and my siblings still needed to attend school.

After spending a few days in the shelter, Mama turned to the option that she had been avoiding for so long; returning back to South Carolina. While we were at the laundry mat washing clothes, she called my aunt who was living in Boiling Springs, SC at the time and asked if we could come there and stay to help her get back on her feet. My aunt and her husband said yes, and up highway 85 northbound to South Carolina we went.

"A loss ain't a loss, it's a lesson. Appreciate the pain, it's a blessing." - Jay-Z ● ● ●

Many people often get baffled when I tell them that I'm actually thankful for everything that has happened in the past. They normally reply with, "What? So, you're thankful that you went to jail?! You're thankful that you experienced being homeless?!"

As a matter of fact, I'm so thankful that I feel blessed! With the direction that I was headed in life, if I didn't go to jail and "wake up" when I did, then I probably would be dead right now. If we didn't lose everything, go homeless, and move when we did, then we probably would still be struggling right now with no control of our finances. I wouldn't have learned valuable life lessons; lessons that I am discussing in this book.

A lot of people who grew up like me actually had great intentions and drive to get out of the environments we were in, but drive without direction leads young black people such as me, to an unforgiving judicial system. A felony can make a situation worse because jobs won't take a chance on felons, even if they have been free for twenty years. A lot of us actually aren't criminals; we just became good at a lot of bad things while chasing success and wanting a life better than we were given.

I'm blessed because those early life experiences gave me wisdom and helped me grow. While I don't have any awards or anything from my past achievements to show, I gained something much more valuable than any award; a strong family bond, a wife, and two beautiful daughters. I am determined to create a life for my household family opposite of what I experienced in my past; and to ensure that, I must continue to grow and develop as a man, husband, and father, daily.

By the grace of God, I have risen above a past that was filled with lots of pain. I have recreated myself from the inside and out. I have chosen to put away bad habits and thoughts. The crazy part is that I'm not even who I am yet (read that again). I've come a long way, but I still have a ways to go because I elevate every day.

Going through homelessness in the midst of facing a possible 20-year sentence in prison, and not knowing if you're going to be with your family or not was a scary experience for me. I got convicted of the charges. I successfully served my felony probation time, and I've been a true free man for about seven years now. I successfully completed my GED and went to college (I didn't finish college, but for a good reason). Those experiences were some of the most humbling experiences ever. Having those experiences is the reason why I'm 27 and have so much wisdom.

I used to be filled with anger because I didn't have a relationship with my dad growing up. I used to wish for that father-son relationship. I used to wish that he was at my games. I used to wish that I didn't have to witness him abusing my mother and locking us in the house while he went to work when I was a young boy. I used to wish that he taught me how to become a man. I used to wish for a lot of things to be done differently, but that's the past, and that's behind us. The things that I used to wish for, I now have the opportunity to do for my children. Today, my father and I have a great relationship, and he takes joy in being there for his grandchildren. I love my father just as much as I love my mother. The past is not our residence. We don't live there anymore.

One thing that you must absolutely know is that while you are on your journey, you will indeed go through storms or be faced with setbacks from time-to-time. Adversity will hit you in life, and sometimes when you least expect it. Adversity has no age, gender, or race restrictions. Adversity can happen to anyone of any age at any time. So, the question is not IF you get hit with a setback, but WHEN you get hit with a setback, how will you respond?

I have made tremendous progress since going through my painful experiences in my youth and teenage years. I graduated with my GED in 2011 (the same year as my high school class). I've been convicted, put on felony probation, and successfully completed that probation in 2013. I've started and dropped out of college. I've gotten married and fathered two beautiful daughters. I've worked at four different companies. I've written a book (this is my first one, and I have many more to come!). I've started my own company, and currently, I am in the process of starting my trucking company. I've grown a lot overall as a young man to get to where I am today.

My release from probation in 2013 is when all of this progress really started to take place. We are now in 2020, so I have covered a lot of ground within the last seven years, and I'm still in my twenties. As far as I'm concerned, I'm going to only keep elevating!

So, as I close out this chapter, let me remind you that you too can rise up from anything. You can completely recreate yourself

Nothing is permanent. You will make mistakes, but the key is to learn from those mistakes. You can think new thoughts. You can learn something new. You can create new habits. All that matters is that you continue to elevate, and never go back to live in your past; just reference back to it for motivation. One important requisite to success in any area of your life is to make sure you are at peace with your past. Never be a prisoner of your past. It was just a lesson, not a life sentence. There are no wins and losses; only wins and lessons.

I hope that whatever is hurting you or whatever you are constantly stressing about gets better. May the dark thoughts, the overthinking, and the doubt exit your mind from this moment forward. May clarity replace confusion. May peace and calmness fill your life.

#SuccessIsMyPreyChallenge: Take a moment to reference (not reside) back over your past and ask yourself the following:

- What lessons have I learned from my previous life experiences?
- Am I applying those lessons today?
- Am I in a better position today than I was in the past?
- Is something from the past holding me back from success in any area of my life?
- Am I at peace with my past?

Chapter 3

Imagine Your Success

"You've got to use your imagination to change the situation."- John Henry

Go Back To Your Childhood...

You can learn a lot just from watching a child play and how he or she uses their mind. In fact, you can learn a lot by looking back at your own childhood. Before you reached the age you're at now, do you remember how curious you used to be? Do you remember how creative you used to be? Do you remember your childhood dreams and imaginations? Do you remember your goals and things you wanted to do when you got older? Let's take a trip down memory lane, shall we?

Your imagination is one of the first things that you developed as a child. When you played with your toys, you were using your imagination. When you were running around your parents' house playing superhero, you were using your imagination. When you played outside with your friends you were using your imagination. Whether you realize it or not, your imagination has always been a part of you.

I remember when I was younger, my imagination used to run wild. For example, I used to be very obsessed with eighteen wheelers (confession: I still am). I used to have a backpack filled with toy eighteen wheelers, and I used to literally imagine myself driving inside of those toy eighteen wheelers. I would make the sounds that eighteen wheelers make. I would pretend that I was backing into a loading dock and made the "beep beep" back up sound. I used to be in my room, on my floor, and by myself with nothing but eighteen wheelers and imagination.

Another example is when my friends and I used to ride our bikes around the neighborhood. We always wanted dirt bikes and motorcycles, but we found out real quick, that wasn't going to happen until we got old enough to buy our own. Our parents didn't have any money to buy us any dirt bikes. However, what we did do is put a soda can on the back of our bicycle tire and imagine that we were riding dirt bikes. We didn't have a real dirt bike, but with our imagination, you couldn't tell us that we weren't having fun on our "bicycle dirt bikes."

As I grew from a young lad into a teenager, my imagination started to shift from toys and bikes to flights and a better life. I had imaginations that I wanted to fulfill. I used to imagine myself being a business owner of a great company. I would imagine myself building a company, taking care of great people that I hire, making customers happy, and living a pretty good life that was opposite of how I was growing up. I used to watch *CSI: Miami* when it was on TV, and that's when I started imagining myself going to Miami and traveling the world. I also imagined myself being the greatest father to my future children because I knew what it felt like to not have an active father in my young life, and I didn't want my future children to experience that.

Right now as I type this, I am proud to say that I opened my first business in 2017 (THE J.ANDERS BRAND™). I am also proud to say that I am gearing up to open a transportation company and will be putting 18 wheelers on the road soon!

Today, I can say that I've visited Miami multiple times. In fact, I think the state of Florida is my second home because I've visited other parts of that beautiful state. I am also traveling to other places that I imagined going to when I was younger.

Lastly, I am extremely proud to say that I am a father of two beautiful daughters named Ashyra and Kamirah. I strive to be the father of the year every year of their lives. And in addition to my daughters, I am also a happily married man to a beautiful woman who happens to be their mother.

I have achieved these gifts in life and much more by first imagining myself doing those things. I turned those wild imaginations into reality. The more I imagine, the more motivated I get about bringing those imaginations to life.

According to the Merriam-Webster dictionary, the word imagination is defined as: "the act or power of forming a mental image of something not present to the senses; creative ability." Therefore, if you form a mental image of your future, you will be using your imagination. Imagination is a form of mental art. You and I both have the ability to create whatever we want.

Whenever you hear a story, your mind will automatically try to illustrate what you are hearing. That's your imagination working. You have probably dreamed of all the things you would do if you ever hit the lottery. That's your imagination working. As you can see, whether you know it or not, you use your imagination every day subconsciously. My goal here is to bring it to your awareness, and help you turn your creative imagination into a reality.

Whichever areas of your life that you are seeking success, imagine yourself achieving success in those areas first. If you want to lose weight, imagine how your future body will look. If you want to work for yourself, imagine yourself owning a business. If you want to become a model, imagine yourself walking down a runway at a fashion show in New York. If you want to be an artist, imagine having your artwork on display at art shows. Whatever you want to do, just imagine yourself doing it, and don't stop holding on to that imagination until you achieve exactly what you imagined.

Remember, you were once a child and your imagination used to run wild. Remember those crazy big dreams you had? Get back to dreaming and imagining your life on a bigger scale. I understand that you are an adult now, and that you have to focus on the adult life and pay bills and whatnot, but I want you to think back on your past imaginations; think back to the things you used to dream about. What happened to those dreams and imaginations?

Don't be afraid to dream some new dreams and imagine the future that you want to create for yourself from where you are today. Don't be afraid to think and dream big. Don't worry about what *can't* happen when there's so much that *can* happen. Imagine the life that you want you and your children to have someday.

So many people die without living out their true potential, because they settle for mediocrity. So many people die with multi-million dollar ideas, because they never executed them. So many people stress every day and allow life to whip them. So many people die at the age 25 but are not buried until they're 85, because they stopped imagining; they stopped dreaming and working towards those dreams that they once had!

It is extremely important that you imagine your way to success in any area of your life that you are seeking success. Paint a mental image in your mind of how you want your future to be, and don't stop working until you are living out those imaginations.

In interviews, some interviewers would ask the successful interviewee a question such as, "Did you ever imagine being this successful?" Most of the time, the interviewee will say something like, "No, I've never imagined myself being this successful in life." Well, when I get interviewed, I'm not downplaying my success. I'll be answering with a firm, "Yes, I imagined all of this years ago!"

#SuccessIsMyPreyChallenge: Take time in the morning and at night before bed to dwell on your future. Take these moments to imagine your success. After imagining your success in the mornings, you should find yourself attacking your day with high energy and enthusiasm. After imagining your success at night, you may find yourself having the most positive dreams and a good night sleep!

Chapter 4

Upgrade

"Check yourself before you wreck yourself."- Ice Cube

If you take a look around, you may notice that you see a lot of people who are on what I like to call the "hamster wheel cycle of life." The life of an average adult goes as follows: go to work, get off work, watch TV, eat, shower, and repeat it all over the next day. On their off days, they don't do much of anything. So many people are going nowhere fast. So many people have settled for mediocre. They are just trying to survive until their time is up on earth. They don't have the motivation to strive and upgrade their life.

Some people lack motivation because they are content right where they are. They figure that going to work to only pay bills and die is good enough. Those are the people that will say things like, "I may be broke, but at least my bills are paid."

The main problem that I have isn't even the fact that they are content. The real problem is that they spend so much time complaining about their life, but yet, they are not doing anything to upgrade their life. You may have found yourself in this same cycle. I know I was once in the vicious cycle of complaining and making excuses every day. However, if I wanted to elevate in life, I had to cut those complaints and excuses, and upgrade myself.

You upgrade your phone, right?

I'm a huge Apple fan, so it's a no brainer that I'm "Team iPhone." I've had just about every iPhone, up until the iPhone 6 (I skipped the 7 and currently have the iPhone 8). Every two years when a new upgrade would be released, I would be right there to get it, even if I didn't *need* it. The truth is, I didn't need those upgrades as soon as they were released. I made myself believe that I needed those upgrades just to keep up with the status quo. I felt like a "big shot" around my peers every time I upgraded to the latest iPhone model (immaturely stroking my ego).

One day, I walked into Verizon and was about to upgrade to the iPhone 7, but I quickly stopped myself when a reality hit me. I asked myself, *Man, what are you doing?* I *wanted* the iPhone 7, but the reality was that I didn't necessarily *need* the iPhone 7. I realized in that moment how quick I was to upgrade my cell phone but hadn't even upgraded myself.

I was spending $800 for a phone but was stopping by Wendy's to get a four for $4 meal almost every other day. I was upgrading to the latest phone but wasn't upgrading my health.

I was upgrading my phone, but I wasn't upgrading my skills to add to my resume. I was spending a massive number of hours a day on my upgraded phone, but I wasn't spending anytime improving my physical and mental health.

Physical Health and Mental Wellness

Physical Health

I have learned in my very own experience that in order to obtain and maintain success in any area of life, you must frequently upgrade *your* operating system, just as you would do with your cell phone or anything else. There are two major factors that contribute to your operation as a human being: your physical health and your mental wellness. We'll discuss both factors and how they both play a role in how you operate.

Let's start with the physical health factor. Everyone wants good health, but they think they have to trade it for success. Contrary to popular belief, I don't think one has to trade their health in order to become successful at whatever it is they are focused on. You'll hear success stories from people that say things like, "I sacrificed by eating oodles and noodles every day, so that I could get to where I am today." You may have also heard, "I sacrificed sleep so that I could build my dreams." I agree that along your journey, you have to make sacrifices, but sleep shouldn't be one the sacrifices.

I believe taking your health seriously is an important component to your success journey. Your rest, eating habits, exercise habits, and overall lifestyle habits, all play pivotal roles in your ability to obtain and sustain success. Your body has about eleven different systems that work 24/7 to keep you alive, healthy, and well. However, if you don't take care of those systems, you may start experiencing significant health problems.

Stop for a second and think about the generations before you. You may notice that many are dealing with some kind of health issue, whether it's diabetes, cancer, bone and joint problems, heart issues, etc. Besides being born with conditions that are out of our control, some of our issues that we have later in life do not just happen. They are results from our poor habits over the course of our lives, and as our body gets older, it gets weaker; making it harder to fight off internal health problems.

Let's say I consume a lot of alcohol and die from liver poising, then whose fault is that? If I smoke tobacco and/or do drugs, then what do I expect to happen to my health? If I continue to eat a lot of fatty and greasy foods, what do I expect to happen to my health? What happens if I don't stretch my body and exercise regularly? Based on my habits today, where do you think my health will be when I become that "older generation"?

As long as I can help myself, I'm striving to be that 80+ year old man with a sharp mind and youthful energy. I'm not trying to pick on anyone with health issues or turn you into a vegan or anything. I just want to bring awareness to the fact that our health is extremely important, and it's a key component of our overall success journey. Many of us, however, focus on how much money we can make in our lifetime, and while money is extremely important, our health is much more valuable.

I'm not afraid to admit that I wasn't making my health a priority for a while. I wasn't going to get annual checkups. I wasn't stretching or exercising regularly. I wasn't watching what I was eating. In fact, my mentality was, "I'm young, skinny, and never been admitted into the hospital since the day I was born, so I'm healthy." The truth of the matter is, I didn't realize how *dangerously* I was living.

Thankfully, I'm glad to have found a woman who's big on natural health and helps keep me on track with my health. It's like I live with my very on doctor. So now, I have no excuse not to make my health a priority. Not only has my diet *upgraded*, but my mentality towards health has also *upgraded* because of her. Many of us are reactive rather than being proactive. The mentality that I once had was a reactive mindset. I wasn't being proactive with my health. I was simply living like most people live. I was just chasing "success" and living a poor unhealthy lifestyle. Subconsciously, I was living life for the moment, and not for the future.

Like some people, I don't like hospitals, and did not like going to visit doctors. However, now with my *upgraded* mindset, I make sure to schedule an annual checkup/physical with my doctor. With my *upgraded* mindset, I'm eating healthier and exercising more. With my *upgraded* mindset, I'm now getting my proper sleep every night (yes, sleeping and resting is important to your health). I'm not going to wait until I get older with health problems to start taking my health more serious. Yes, I'm only 27, but I made a commitment to myself to remain proactive with my health for the rest of my life.

You should make sure that your systems within your body are working well, so that you will be able to gain and maintain success on your journey. Taking care of your health is also success. Heath is True wealth. After all, what's the point of having success if you are spending the majority of your time being sick and unhealthy to even enjoy your success?

The motto "get rich or die trying" is a bogus motto in my opinion. I'm not saying don't focus on making money or anything, because money is definitely important (we'll discuss that in chapter 6). If money is your motivation, then by all means go for it. I'm just saying don't *kill* yourself trying to become *rich* in this world. Don't put your health on the back burner just for a dollar or a dream. Live in reality and take care of your health to the best of your ability while in pursuit of your dreams and goals. You should be actively upgrading and maintaining good health. You will realize that no amount of money is worth risking your health. You have no excuse to not take care of your health!

Mental Wellness

Your mental wellness is the other major factor that contributes to your operation as a human being. Your mind never stops working because you have two minds: a conscious and a subconscious mind. Your subconscious mind is working when your conscious mind isn't (i.e. dreaming while sleeping). Our minds are always thinking, working, and recording things 24/7.

It's important to understand just how powerful our minds are. With our minds, we create our lives. With our minds we make decisions daily. With our minds, we either produce good or bad; positive or negative into the world. Because our minds are so powerful, and just like we have to be careful what we feed our bodies, we must also be careful about what we "feed" our minds.

What we ingest into our minds regularly has an impact on our life in some way, shape, or form. I'm pretty sure you have heard the saying, "If you can believe it, you can achieve it." That quote isn't just catchy, it's very true. Everything that I've achieved thus far in my young life isn't by accident. Everything that you do in life, whether good or bad, is a reflection of your mind state.

As I stated earlier in the book, besides the environment that I grew up in playing a huge role in some of my past negative actions, the music that I consumed didn't make things any better. Listening to "Wasted" by Gucci Mane, and "Steady Mobbin" by him and Lil Wayne had me really wilding and living a dangerous lifestyle, because I was really trying to live what they were rapping about. Their music had a negative impact on my mind, and I didn't even know it.

Today, I listen to and read things that uplift my mental state. I do what some may consider as boring. I listen to podcasts, uplifting music, and read educational material. I don't smoke, drink, or club hop anymore. Don't get me wrong, I still enjoy hip-hop because I'm a fan of art (I enjoy all music), so I can listen to hip-hop from an art perspective and vibe with the motivational content provided by a few artists.

Again, I'm not knocking or trying to belittle anyone who does those things, nor am I trying to force you to do what I do, but I've elevated my mind and evolved as a person, and I just choose not to indulge in those activities. If it's not making my mind and my health better, and not helping me *upgrade,* then I don't need it in my life. I don't need it in my space. I don't need it in my environment.

Does that make me better than the next person? No, it

certainly does not. But when you know better, you move better.

The point is: you don't accidentally become successful. You succeed by consciously creating success in your mind. You succeed by keeping your mind in a positive environment. You succeed by upgrading your mind which helps upgrade your *operating system.*

In this technology-driven era and materialistic world that we are living in, we are constantly upgrading. We are constantly upgrading our cell phones, our cars, and our wardrobes, just to name a few. Those things are great to upgrade, but when is the last time you upgraded yourself? When is the last time you upgraded your skills? When is the last time you updated your resume? How often do you upgrade your mental state? Your body has many different systems that are working 24/7. How often do you upgrade your operating system? Upgrading your operating system, which is you, is imperative for your elevation towards success.

You must be actively upgrading. Continue to sharpen your mind. Make your overall health a priority. An unhealthy lifestyle can and will affect your mental state, and if you seek success, you can't afford to compromise your mind and your health along the journey.

I'm not saying don't upgrade your cell phone, because I can assure you that I'll still be upgrading mine when *needed*. I'm just saying, don't upgrade your cell phone, and not be working on upgrading yourself at all. That's pretty much like living backwards (which we'll also discuss later). In order to elevate, you must trade poor habits for good habits that will help you *upgrade* and get you to success.

So, how do you *upgrade*? Here are a few tips that have worked for me, as well as for other "successful" people that I have studied:

- Continue to learn new material and skills
- Maintain a positive environment: only place yourself around positive environments.
- Network: Join groups, make friends, and have a positive support system that is encouraging you to upgrade.
- Watch the activities that you engage in: remember, negative activities aren't helping your health or your mind upgrade.
- Reflect and meditate daily: Find a nice quiet place that you can call your "peace zone."
- Take a break from the grind: be sure to create "rest" time into your schedule, as it is important to give your mind a break, and it is also important for your health!
- Remain conscious of your habits: remember, poor habits lead to poor results in life, and you weren't put on this earth to be poor.
- Seek mentorship: having mentors in my life who challenge me has been a major key to helping me *upgrade!*

"Your next level is going to demand a better

you. So upgrade!"

Chapter 5

What's More Valuable

Than Money?

"Name all the valuable assets that you have, and if you

don't mention time, then you don't have anything."

- J.ANDERS

Some people will say that your twenties are supposed to be your young, wild, and free years. You know how it goes: party every weekend, drink like a goldfish, smoke like a chimney, sex everyone that you can, buy out the mall, etc. That's what some older guys used to tell me when I mentioned how young I was and that I was married. When I was younger than I am now, and mentioned that I was married in my twenties, their initial reaction would be, "Man, when I was in my twenties, I was living life! This is what I was doing…" I used to sit back and listen to them brag about how "wild" their twenties were.

However, I took notice on their position in life at that current moment, and I also took heed to their regrets. They didn't have a lot to show at that time in their lives, and soon after they finished their bragging stories, they would go into their regrets. The number one thing they often told me usually went something along the lines of, "But young man, I'm proud of you and where your head is at in your twenties, because if I could go back to my twenties and do it all over again, I would have taken my time much more seriously."

The key word that stood out the most when I heard their regrets is the word TIME. I study, talk, and listen to individuals who have built success for themselves in their own way; and I also study, talk, and listen to people who haven't quite lived up to their full potential. One of the biggest differences between the two groups I found is how they managed their time.

Time Flies

How many times have you started the year in January, and before you know it, it's time to have another new year's celebration? How many times do you say to yourself, "Man, time is flying!" or "where has time gone?" I know I say it a lot myself. I remember what an older guy named Keith told me during my freshman year of high school. He said, "Enjoy these four years of high school, because once you graduate, you'll be turning 40 before you know it." I know Keith wasn't lying, because here I am now, only two and a half years away from turning 30!

As I stated in chapter 2, I have made tremendous progress with my life since getting in trouble and completing my probation in 2013. I'm thankful for making those mistakes young in life rather than making those mistakes later and much older in life. I knew if I wanted to elevate my life, then I had to take my time serious while I am still young.

You are the CEO

It was brought to my attention in college, in one of my management courses, that we are all managers of life before we are managers of any business. Many of us tend to overlook the importance of managing unless we have "manager" in our job title. We want to be managers at a company, but don't have a system in place for managing everyday life. We want to own businesses and be CEOs, but what about managing our household first? Just because you may or may not be a manager at your job doesn't mean you're exempt from managing life.

The truth is, you are the Chief Executive Officer (CEO) of YOUR life; so why not learn management skills that can make you a better manager of your life, and possibly even help you land a management position in a company or help you manage your own company someday? I think life and business go hand-in-hand. I don't think one can effectively manage a business if they aren't effectively managing their life.

While there are many different skills that can help one become a great manager, my focus here is on one of the most important skills; time management. The reason why I am focusing so much on time management is because I feel that many of us don't take it very seriously, or in most cases, we wait until it's too late. Time can be your best friend or your worst enemy, depending on how you use it.

Let's look at some facts about time. You and I both get the same amount of time every year and every day. We both get the same 365 days a year. We both get the same 8,760 hours a year. We both get the same 525,600 minutes a year. We both get the same 168 hours a week. We both get the same 10,080 minutes a week. I say all of that just to say we both get the same 24 hours a day, and 7 days a week, which is why I don't buy into the "I don't have time" excuse that people love to make as the reason for not elevating in life.

I understand that we all have different situations in life, so everyone's time usage may vary, but over the next few pages, we'll explore how a person who doesn't control their time spends their time (average) versus how a person who controls their time spends their time (elite).

Here's a quick scenario of the average person's lifestyle. They work 40 hours a week at their job. They sleep 8 hours per night which totals up to 56 hours a week. 42 hours goes towards eating, family, and television. They are now left with about 30 hours in the week, and we haven't even included the amount of time that they're on social media each week, or anything else that they spend time on.

The average individual is living in the hamster wheel cycle. They repeat the same everyday activities. They sleep in late and don't really use any time to set and work towards goals, but those 30 hours, however, will determine whether they elevate or not.

More than likely, they'll spend the majority (if not all) of those 30 hours idling on social media, looking at some nonsense stuff or talking about how "bored" they are and binge watch Netflix shows. In fact, I read an article on MarketWatch in 2018 that discussed how people spend most of their waking hours staring at screens.

A paragraph from the article reads, *"According to a new study by market-research group Nielsen, American adults spend more than 11 hours per day watching, reading, listening to, or simply interacting with media. 62% of that time is attributed to app/web browsing on smartphones."* 11 hours a day times 7 days is 77 hours a week, and that's pretty much equivalent to working a 12-hour shift at a job. It doesn't take much to see how that study can be true. Before moving to our next example, let me elaborate a little more on the above scenario.

Despite how light our phones are in our hands, they hold big weight in our everyday activities. Take a look at yourself and society around you, and you will notice just how engaged we all are in our phones. More than likely, Facebook, Instagram, or Snapchat is on the screens of our phones.

Don't misunderstand me here. I am not against social media, smartphones or anything, because I use social media and my phone daily like you as well. The difference with me now is that I'm more aware of HOW I utilize my time on my phone. When I wasn't as productive or time conscious as I am now, I used to catch myself idling and strolling on social media for hours at a time. I fell well into that study by Nielsen.

It wasn't until I started to value my time the same way I value my money that I saw positive results starting to happen in my life.

"If you start treating time like money, then maybe you won't throw it away. After all, time is money, and neither can be wasted."

I'm sure you've heard the phrase "time is money." That is a very true statement. What's also true is that wasted time is the worst thing you could waste. It's not about how much you sleep, it's about what you do when you're awake that determines how far you will elevate. If you're bored at 2 a.m. asking Facebook "Who's up with me?" then you may need to look into redirecting your time. If you're not doing anything productive outside of your job on your days off, then you may need to look into redirecting your time.

The fact is this: REAL HUSTLERS AND GRINDERS ARE NEVER BORED. REAL HUSTLERS AND GRINDERS UNDERSTAND TIME MANAGEMENT AND HOW TO PLAN AND MOVE STRATEGICALLY!

I honestly can't even remember the last time I was bored. If you are always bored, then to me, that means you have too much idle time on your hands. Don't be complaining about your situation when you could use that "boring" time to be productive in elevating your future. If you're not where you want to be in life, then why exactly are you bored? Why aren't you working on elevating? You keep telling yourself that you want to elevate in life, but the truth is, you don't want it bad; you just "kind of want it."

Instead of posting "Who's up with me? I'm bored" on Facebook at 2 a.m., maybe you could ask for recommendations on a good book to read. If you notice that you are bored a lot, then find an area of your life that needs some work and get to work. You want better health? Then get active on your diet and exercise. Do you want to build that business? It's not going to be built if you're always bored. There is always an area in your life that can be elevated, so to be honest, you should never be bored.

I read on the internet once that the average worker reads an average of less than one book a year and works an average of 37.5 hours per week. This same person makes 319 times less money than the top U.S. CEOs, who claim to read more than 60 books a year. Do you think Bill Gates, Jeff Bezos, or Steve Jobs built the companies they built because they were bored? No! They were busy elevating!

Do you think Michael Jordan, LeBron James, or Kobe Bryant dominated the game of basketball by being bored? No! While their peers were in the house playing video games, they were on the court working on their game!

Do you think the owners of local restaurants in your community obtained them by being bored? No! They put in work to make their restaurant ideas come to life. Do you think the company that you currently work for was built off of boredom? No! It was built because the founder(s) had a vision and worked to make that vision come alive! Do you think my company will be built by me sitting around bored? No! As I stated earlier, I honestly can't remember the last time I was bored. I use my time efficiently to elevate!

What about a break?

I know it may seem like I'm saying that all you should do is work, work, work, and take no breaks. No, that is definitely not the point here. In fact, I encourage you to take breaks each week. As I stated in chapter 4, not only does your body need breaks, it's important for your health. Downtime/rest time is very much needed when you're on your *success* journey, but there is a difference between being bored and having strategic downtime.

Here's the difference. Being bored is uncalculated time whereas downtime or rest time is calculated time. Downtime or rest time should be calculated within your schedule. Utilize your downtime however you like, as long as it's reserved within your schedule. The tricky thing about downtime is that if you are not careful, it can quickly turn into idle time, so that's why it's important to plan your time.

Aim to get a system in place so that you can utilize your time with as much structure as possible. The more structure you have with your time, the more you will position yourself for more success and elevation along your journey.

Time and Goals

One thing I've learned from studying the "elite" people who control their time is that they plan their time around their goals, and they are very strategic about it. This is something that I have applied as well. I utilize my time according to the goals that I have set. I write down my goals, and then attach dates to those goals. Once I attach ideal dates that I seek to achieve my goals, I then plan out my schedule so that it will put me on track to hit those goals. Some goals are "automatic life goals"(as I like to call them) such as: having quality family time, my exercise routine, scheduling time with friends, rest time, growing my company, education, team meetings, vacation travel, etc.

Some of my other goals are my "end date goals" such as: completing projects, purchasing a home, new product launch in my business, graduating college, completing a book, etc. I have made it a habit to plan my time around my goals, and by doing that, it has allowed me to manage my time with more structure.

Game planning

When it actually comes to planning my schedule, I go through five phases. First and foremost, I have a 5-year plan mapped out with goals I seek to achieve. I plan by the year, quarter, month, and week.

First, towards the end of a year, I start planning for the next upcoming year. I set goals or projects that I'm working on or will start working on that I look to achieve or make progress on within the next year.

Secondly, with those yearly goals written down, I then break those goals down into quarterly goals. The quarterly goals act as little progress checkpoints for the actual goal(s) that I am working towards. The yearly and quarterly phases are planned out before the next year starts.

Third, once the quarterly goals are written down, I then move on to the monthly phase. The monthly phase is where I'll start a little more micromanaging. Towards the end of each month, I start getting my schedule prepared for the following month. This is where I would go ahead and fill in dates with appointments and goals that must get accomplished that month that will help towards the quarterly goals.

Finally, once I have filled in my calendar for the month, I am now moving on to the weekly phase. Every Sunday, I take about 15 minutes or less to just simply review the following week. I update or tweak my schedule on a weekly basis if needed.

I know all of this may seem like a lot, but stick with me. Honestly, it's actually easy. Remember, the first two phases are done before you start your new year when you set any goals that you plan to achieve within the next year. The monthly phase is done at the end of each month. Because you would have already filled in your weeks in the monthly phase, the weekly phase is just a quick review of each upcoming week.

What also makes planning easy is that your automatic life goals would be the first to go into your schedule. They are your automatic goals because those are the most important goals in your life. Spending time with my family is an automatic life goal. My health is an automatic life goal. Regardless of anything that I have going on in life, I must make sure I have time built into my schedule for my family, and I make time for taking care of my health and wellness. After you have planned out time for your automatic life goals you will then find it easy to input the rest of your priorities.

By planning your time around your goals, you will discover that you will not have any boring or idle time in your schedule. The key is stay busy, but busy in a good way. You want to be as productive as possible with your time. You don't want to be busy doing nothing. You don't want to be busy going nowhere fast. You want to be busy producing positive results and elevating your life.

Once again, I cannot stress enough to not get totally caught up with being overwhelmingly busy. Be sure to build rest/downtime into your schedule. I used to sacrifice my health by not even sleeping or eating as I should have been. I used to think that I had to be "all work and no play." When I started really studying the "elite group," that's when I found out that life is a marathon, and not a sprint! Once I realized that, my whole perspective changed on the way I was working and utilizing my time. Now, let's dive into how the elite control their time.

High performance coach and author, Brendon Burchard wrote in his book, *High Performance Habits:*

"There's something frustrating about working hard, being passionate and grateful, and still not advancing, still not feeling it. There's also something depleting about it all; excelling sometimes but feeling exhausted too often; having grit and getting paid but not feeling rewarded; being motivated but not creating real momentum; engaging with others but not really connecting; adding value but not making a dent. That's not a vision of life we desire."

Bruchard also said, *"As it turns out, high performers' sustained success is due to their healthy approach to living. It's not just about achievement in a profession or in just one area of interest. It's about creating a life in which you experience an ongoing feeling in full engagement, joy, and confidence that comes from being your best self. Lots of people have amazing personal strengths, but destroy their health in their quest for success, and thus, can't maintain high performance."*

I couldn't have agreed more with those statements by Mr. Bruchard. I was that person who was "busy" but wasn't seeing any real results. I was that person who lacked vision and wasn't building my time around my goals. I was that person who was destroying my health in quest for "success." It doesn't matter how many millions I accumulate or what area I'm aiming for success in, if I'm not mentally and physically healthy, then what have I achieved?

My point is this: yes, you want to be busy, but you also want to make sure that you are being productive, and not just being busy going nowhere fast. You want to make sure that you are not harming yourself or anyone else in your quest for success. And finally, as Bruchard puts it once again, "I care that you succeed and have a healthy life full of positive emotions and relationships."

With that being said, let me share an example of how an elite individual utilizes and controls their time, and how they elevate in life.

Let's take billionaire Jack Dorsey, founder and CEO of companies Twitter and Square, as an example. Mr. Dorsey is indeed a billionaire, and you would think that he would drive an exotic car to his office, or have a chauffeur drop him off each morning. Jack Dorsey wakes up at 5 a.m. and walks 5 miles to work every morning. During the 5-mile walk, he unplugs. He takes that time to listen to music and audio books, or simply to think and draw inspiration from the streets he is walking. He told author Tim Ferris in the book *Tools of Titans* (which is a great book by the way) that taking time to walk to work every day is the most worthwhile investment he's ever made. Mr. Dorsey is just one of many examples of how he utilizes his time efficiently and also makes his health a priority.

The Four Ds

I want to share one last point with you as I close out this chapter. To effectively make the most of managing your time, you must have the four Ds. The four Ds are: Desire, Decisiveness, Determination, and Discipline. To give you a quick breakdown of the four Ds, I'll share with you how world-renowned speaker and successful business man Brian Tracy explains it.

Mr. Tracy says, "You must have an intense, burning **desire** to get your time under control and to achieve maximum effectiveness. You must make a clear **decision** that you are going to practice good time management techniques until they become a habit. You must have **determination** and be willing to persist in the face of all temptations to the contrary until you become an effective time manager. And finally, the most important key to success in life, you must **discipline** yourself to make time management a lifelong practice."

Becoming a great manager of your time is vital to your success in life. Remember, I get the same 168 weekly hours, and the same 24 daily hours as you do. Don't waste time by hiding behind the "I don't have time" excuse. The truth is you DO have time. You make time for what's important to you. Obviously, we can't do everything at once, so don't overwhelm yourself trying to cram all of your goals in at once. Again, it's a marathon, not a sprint.

**If you are older, don't you dare think for one second that you don't have any time left to elevate your life. The retail store that you shop at called Walmart was founded by Sam Walton when he was 45 years old. Colonel Sanders didn't find Kentucky Fried Chicken (KFC) until he was 65 years old. You are never too old to elevate your life. Start managing your time better, starting today, and you will start to see the difference tomorrow.

If you are in your 20s like me, or younger, please remember that you have one huge advantage and that's having time on your side. Use the time you have now to build your future. Listen and learn from the older generation when they start talking out of regret, and how they wish they had taken their future more seriously. Sure, you can have fun, and please do. I encourage you to do so. I'm not telling you to be uptight or to put yourself on a leash. I'm just saying, don't get carried away and let precious time slip away.

Personally, I don't want to look back 20 plus years from now and still be stuck in the same place mentally, physically, spiritually, and financially. That's why I make it a point to take my time serious, and to manage my time effectively. When young people ask me 20 years from now for advice, and how I got into the position that I will be in, I will say, "Well, this is what I did in my 20s...." I don't want to talk to them out of regret. I want to talk to them out of success, and show them that they can also achieve greatness in life if they take care of their time while they are young.

Remember, depending on how you use it, time can be your biggest asset or your biggest waste. If you don't take the time to work on creating a life you want, you will eventually be forced to spend a lot of time dealing with a life you don't want. The earlier you start, the more time you have to mess up and learn from your mistakes. I've failed early, but I also turned those Ls into lessons and learned early. You are CEO of your life. Take control of your time.

#SuccessIsMyPreyChallenge Ask yourself the following:

How can I improve my time management?

What are my goals and priorities?

What areas can I cut back with my time?

What areas do I need to put more time towards?

"He or she who makes the most of his or her time will accomplish the most. Become a master of the clock; not a slave to it."

Chapter 6

Bag Talk

"Money can't buy happiness, and poverty can't buy anything."- *Grant Cardone*

In this chapter, I want to discuss the next most valuable thing in your life. Let's talk about something that you and I both use daily. Let's talk about something that you and I can't live without. Let's talk about something that flows through our hands like water. Let's talk about something that we get up and go to work for. Let's talk about money. Let's discuss financial literacy. Let's discuss getting the "bag," maintaining and protecting the bag, and passing the bag down to the next generation.

Hip-hop artist, Drake, said in a song, "People with no money act like money isn't everything." That line sums up the fact that most people who say "money isn't everything" are people who most likely do not have a great deal of wealth. Many of us have adopted the mentality that money isn't everything, primarily because many of us grew up in poverty with no money. It's easy to say that when you're living below the poverty line.

I do agree that money isn't everything (meaning money shouldn't be the only thing we care about in life), but I will say money is an important tool, a very important tool. Without money, our bills wouldn't get paid. Without money, we wouldn't be able take ourselves and our children on nice vacations. Without money, we wouldn't be able to feed our children. Without money, we can't survive, thrive, or elevate ourselves nor our families. Money has been around for centuries, so as far as I'm concerned, money plays a huge role in our lives whether we want it to or not.

Financial literacy is something I wish that I was taught at a younger age by my parents, and by the public school system. I think personal finance is something that should be taught to children in every household, starting at young ages, and should be a mandatory curriculum taught in all schools.

Although I wish I was taught financial literacy at a young age, I can't blame my mother for her lack of financial education, because she didn't know what she didn't know. She only did what she knew financially to the best of her knowledge and ability. I also can't necessarily expect the public school system to teach me personal finance, let alone how to build wealth. The public school system isn't designed to teach us how to build wealth. It just prepares us for the workforce out in the world.

Pastors Build Wealth and Live Their Best Lives Too....Why Can't You?

Another mindset and a saying that often gets misconstrued is the saying, "money is the root of all evil." We have tossed that one sentence around so loosely without giving it much consideration as to what it truly means. I challenge that by saying loud and clear that Money is NOT, I repeat, is NOT the root of all evil. Most people seem to think that money is inherently evil, and we should find no delight whatsoever in money. Verse 10 from the book of 1 Timothy actually says, and I quote, "For the LOVE of money is the root of all evil: which while some coveted after, they have erred from the faith, and pierced themselves through with many sorrows" (King James Version).

With a quick glance at the verse, I could understand how someone may think money is *bad*. One may start to feel guilty about making money and enjoying a decent lifestyle after reading that verse. In fact, many of us feel guilty for making money.

The difference between the actual verse and the misconstrued sentence is the word "love." The context in which the word is being used is actually talking about greed, it's talking about covetousness. So, money itself is not a root of all evil, but an unhealthy affection, and a greedy desire for money is.

I fear that this common misconception that money is the root of all evil will lead to what I call poverty theology. I can almost guarantee that T.D. Jakes, Joel Osteen, Dale C.

Bronner, and other multimillionaire preachers do not follow the misconception that money is the root of all evil. These men own businesses, write books, produce movies, speak at events, etc., and just like you and I go to work to get paid, they must get paid as well. They just figured out a path for them to build wealth and a decent lifestyle for them and their families, and they have every right to do so without feeling guilty.

So, does accumulating wealth make preachers, musicians, business owners, etc. around the world evil? No. It's all about one's desires and motives behind the money. Having a lot of money isn't bad. Having greed and love for money more than God, your family, people, and even yourself is where it gets bad. Being a multimillionaire isn't evil, but looking down on those who aren't and treating them like they're not humans is what's evil. Seeking to build wealth for the right reasons is not evil, but any negative (illegal) actions to get that wealth is evil. For example, a spouse killing the other spouse to cash in on a hefty life insurance policy is evil.

Material possessions are not the problem; greed, covetousness, and pride are. As long as you have the right motives, you shouldn't feel bad for saving and investing your money, taking a job for more money, or seeking to make more money for the right reasons. Money is not the root of all evil. Money is a tool, and that's it—just a tool. Feel free to enjoy it, but also seek to steward it wisely. Check your heart to see whether you're the kind of person that has an unhealthy desire for money, because it doesn't end too well for those that do.

So again, money is NOT the root of all evil. Most people believe that subconsciously, so they hinder themselves from financial growth. Change the way you view money, and your relationship with money will change. Now, let's move on to the money rules.

Every Game Has Rules

There's a financial game out here. We must first learn the rules to the game in order to play and win the game in our personal lives. According to a quick google search, there are about 46.8 million multimillionaires around the world. According to a Forbes billionaire list I read in 2019, there are 2,153 billionaires worldwide. Most of us probably only know the famous ones like Jay-Z, Jeff Bezos, Warren Buffet, Bill Gates, and the people that are entertainers and athletes.

There are so many millionaires and billionaires that we don't even know that are living in our very own backyard, and we probably wouldn't know that they are wealthy because they are "hiding in plain sight," dressed in their jogging pants and plain shirts out in public.

I used to be envious of those famous millionaires and billionaires who had all of the money, and I was growing up poor in poverty, until one day as an adult, I thought to myself, *why hate on and envy these people when I can be learning from them? What do these people know that I don't know? They are human just like me, and they are no special than me.* I felt that if they could build wealth, then so could I. I just had to stop being envious of those that were wealthy and start learning the game from them. I wanted to learn some dos and don'ts, and learn from their mistakes. Many wealthy people started from poverty like me, so why wouldn't I want to learn how he or she climbed out of the mud of poverty and gained and sustained the financial success they have achieved?

So, I've been researching and studying the wealthy, and I want to share what I have learned with you as well. The things that they do know are simple, but effective knowledge. Every game has rules, and we are about to explore some rules and knowledge that the wealthy has applied to the financial/life game, and I'm certain that they will help you as well!

Financial rule #1: Be a Student of the Game first.

Most people tend to think that if they made more money, all of their problems would go away. How many times have you said, or have you heard, "I need to hit the lottery!" News flash: no amount of money will ever be enough for someone who is horrible with money or live beyond their means. Taking a job for more money will not solve anything if you still have poor money habits. More money is not the answer; better financial habits are the key.

Instead of always seeking a job that pays more and thinking your problems are going to vanish, opt for financial literacy. You don't know what you don't know, but if you never learn then you'll never know. You can't afford to not educate yourself financially.

Without proper financial literacy, I can almost guarantee that you will end up losing the financial game. Those who are financially educated have more control over their money.

More money doesn't bring them more problems because they know what to do with the money.

Getting a financial education means to learn credit and debt management, interest rates, saving, investing, compound interest, etc. With a solid financial education, you will not act on impulse, make emotional decisions when it comes to your money, and will not be easily taken advantage of financially.

Many people say that they want a million dollars, but yet have no idea what to do with a million dollars besides spend it all. They talk about everything that they are going to *buy*, because they lack financial discipline, and they lack financial discipline because they lack financial education.

The good news is that you don't have to go to an ivy league school or Clemson University to become financially educated. There are financial advisors that can help advise and educate you about your financial decisions. I would highly recommend that you get a financial advisor who has your best interest at heart to help guide you along financially. That has been one of the best decisions I've made, and I'm sure you won't regret having one either.

In addition to having a good financial advisor, you may also find some great financial knowledge by reading books. I've read lots of financial/wealth building books. Some books I agree with, and some I don't, but in all books, I have learned something valuable regardless. Being an avid reader has certainly been a big advantage for me, and it has also paid off for individuals who are financially wealthy in life. Most millionaires/billionaires contribute their financial success to reading books.

The first rule to the financial game is to educate yourself. Don't be busy "chasing the money" and have no understanding of what to do with the money. There is a difference between being busy chasing money and being effective with money. So many people believe that because they are *making* money, they are going to build wealth, and that's certainly not true. Chasing money your whole life without taking time to understand finances is like trying to use a drill tool without taking time to learn how to use it first. You may end up hurting yourself rather than helping yourself.

Financial Rule #2: Change Your Relationship with Money.

Earlier in the book, I talked about how powerful your mind is. I won't go too deep into it again. I just want to reemphasize that if you want to be wealthy then you must be wealthy in the mind first. Constantly discussing how broke you are isn't going to help you become wealthy. Understand that your bank account is only broke if your mentality is broke. Your bank account is a reflection of your relationship with money.

Every individual who has built wealth didn't become wealthy by having a broke mentality. They became wealthy and continue to be wealthy by first being wealthy in their mind. They refuse to settle for anything less than their worth. They understand that they deserve wealth for themselves and their families.

You can't obtain financial wealth with an $18 an hour mentality. As my close friend James Setzer said once, "Your employer decides how much they are going to pay you. They don't decide how much you will make." So if you want to build true financial wealth, stop thinking, 'how much can I make a hour,' and start thinking 'how much income can this asset earn me each month or each year.'"

Stop thinking that it's normal to live broke and in debt just because you may have come up that way. Money is nothing more than a tool, so change the way you view that tool, and your relationship will change with that tool.

Financial Rule #3: Learn to control the game. Build your cash reserves.

You have two choices: it's either you control this financial game, or this game will control you. Although it's a real estate game, there is a lesson that one can learn from the infamous board game, Monopoly. Most people aim to make the most money in the board game, but actually it's the one with the most *control* on the board who ultimately wins the game. In the game chess, the person who takes control is the person who wins. If you are not in control of your finances, then you risk not being in control of your life.

My next example is not to pick on anyone because I'd never want to work without pay, but let's take a look at the government shutdown that kicked the 2019 year off. The federal government shutdown lasted 35 days, and it was the longest federal shutdown in history. For 35 days, federal workers had to work without pay. Most of the country went into panic mode because they were working without pay, but yet, still had to pay bills and maintain life. Some people were just working and may have not been saving any money for a *rainy day*, so they placed themselves in a vulnerable position by not being in control of their finances.

You may or may not work for the federal government, but the same can very well happen to you. Your job can close its doors today, and if you are not in control of your finances, then you put yourself (and your family) at risk of losing the game. If a tornado or hurricane comes through your town and wipes out your house, and you survive, will you be able to make it through that tragic time?

The reality is, by day, many people are trapped in a world of unfulfilling jobs that may disappear tomorrow, and by night, they're buried under the mounting pressure of debt and bills. Many waste years of their lives spinning on a hamster wheel of arbitrary rules and irrational fears. Many defer their freedom to an anticipated 9-5 system controlled by others. Many are wage slaves living paycheck-to-paycheck, and few have saved for a rainy day.

You are not controlling the game if you don't have any money stashed away or growing for you. You are not controlling the game if you are solely relying on your job and living paycheck-to-paycheck. You are not controlling the game if you splurge money on liabilities that depreciate rather than assets that appreciate.

You have the ability to control the financial game in your life in your own way. Don't wait until you're fired, going without pay, or your company decides to close its doors to decide to take control. Build up your savings and have some cash reserved so that you can always be in control of your financial destiny, and be ready for the unexpected in life.

Financial Rule #4: Live Modestly. No Consumption. Stay broke.

Broke people spend money before they get it; the wealthy spend money after they get it. If you spend money before you get it, you'll never have it. You see, a poor individual can only play rich for so long, but a wealthy individual can play broke forever.

Many of us are not emotionally mature when it comes to our money. We see something nice and think that we suddenly have to get it. We'll say things like, "Those Jordans were nice so I just *had* to get them" despite the fact that you already have a closet full of shoes that you barely wear now. Or we will say, "I just *had* to get that new phone because it's nice!" despite the fact that you don't necessarily need a new phone.

The truth is, you didn't "have" to get those shoes or that phone. You allowed your emotions to get the best of you. Lack of emotional maturity will make you broke. If you cannot control your emotions, then you cannot control your money.

If you want to seriously increase your finances, you must learn to live modestly. Don't consume liabilities and stay broke (on purpose). In other words, learn to live within your means. Keeping up with the Joneses will hold you back from financial growth.

To live modestly means to live as frugal as you possibly can while you are building your wealth up. That means to give up the flashy jewelry, cars, and gifts until you have assets that can pay for those things. You may go purchase a pair of $600 Gucci shoes while I'll go buy a nice pair of $10 shoes at a department store.

True story: my wife and I flew down to Miami in the summer of 2016. We went to a nearby mall in the area. Unknowingly, it was one of those expensive high-end malls like Lennox Mall in Atlanta. So as we walked around for a while, we approached a Gucci store. I picked up a pair of Gucci loafers that costed $600 dollars. The interesting thing about the shoes is that they looked identical to the ones I had on my feet! If I didn't tell you what brand shoe they were, you'd probably think I had Gucci on my feet when I walked out of the store. The difference is I purchased my shoes back at home before I even got on the plane for $10 from a store called Maxway. So unknowingly, I had a pair of shoes that looked just like the Gucci shoes, and I paid $590 less.

Gucci doesn't market to me, and I'm perfectly fine with staying in my lane. Gucci markets to those who CAN afford it, but the problem is that it's too many of us buying things that we CANNOT afford just to be seen. The wealthy and the poor put their shoes on their feet for the same purpose, but the difference is that poor minded people don't have assets that can pay for their liabilities, while the wealthy minded have assets that pay for their liabilities.

I can still (and I do) dress very nice without maxing out my credit cards or sending my account in the negative to do so. Warren Buffet, one of the wealthiest billionaires in the world, still lives in the same house he bought in 1958. Jeff Bezos started Amazon out of his garage in 1994. In 1997, he took his company public and became a billionaire, but here's the kicker, he kept driving the same Honda Accord. If you take a good look at most of the millionaires, billionaires, and top CEOs in the world, you will find that they live decent modest lives. They didn't splurge on liabilities before having assets and companies that support the liabilities that they wanted to splurge on.

That brings me to the second phase of this rule. The second phase to this rule is to NOT CONSUME MORE LIABILITIES THAN ASSETS. This is where separating your needs from your wants becomes crucial. And once again, assets are things that help grow your wealth, such as real estate investing, stocks, and businesses. Liabilities are things that take money from your pocket every month, such as car notes, cable bill, shoes, etc. Every purchase you make with your money is either an asset or a liability.

Cars, for example, are one of the biggest liabilities that you could purchase with your credit in my opinion. Why? Well, the second you drive it off the lot, it goes down in value. You may say, "but I need a car." Yea, but do you *need* that 2020 Dodge Charger, or do you *want* that 2020 Dodge Charger? By the time you pay off that car in seven years, you will have paid way more with the interest added on (probably pay double the price with poor credit) and the car would be worth nothing. Unfortunately, most ordinary Americans pay enough in interest and finance charges over their lifetimes to become millionaires if they had the discipline to go save first and then buy, but that's not how they think. Sadly, the mantra in America seems to be "buy now, pay later."

Jay-Z said in a verse, "I bought every V12 engine, wish that I could take it back to the beginning. I could have bought a place in Dumbo before it was Dumbo for like $2 million, that same building today is worth $25 million, guess how I'm feeling, DUMBO."

What Jay-Z is saying is that if he knew back then what he knows now, he wouldn't have bought those cars (liabilities). Instead, he would have bought real estate (asset)! The cars didn't make him any money, whereas the real estate would have made him a ton of money. Jay-Z went from being this flashy young man with all the cars and jewelry, to being the business mogul that he is today because he stopped consuming more liabilities than assets. If you want to build wealth and obtain financial freedom, you need to start increasing your assets and decreasing your liabilities.

The third and final phase to this rule is to STAY BROKE. Don't be broke because you're forced to be broke, but be broke because you *chose* to be broke on purpose. What I mean by that is for you to keep your expenses as low as possible, even while your money is increasing. Just because you receive raises at your jobs doesn't mean you should go out and take on new expenses. If you start off making $18 an hour and now you make $30 an hour, the goal should be to still live like you're making $18 an hour. That excess money should be going to savings and investing. Any bonuses you receive should be going to savings and investing.

People say, "more money equals more problems." That's only because they chose to let more money become a problem. More money shouldn't dramatically change the way you live. It all ties into living modestly and not consuming any liabilities more than assets. If you truly want to obtain financial freedom, then any extra money you have should be invested into something that can produce even more money for you. If your outcome is greater than your income, then you are not helping yourself at all.

Living modestly, having no consumption, and staying broke all stems from living a disciplined lifestyle. If you are disciplined with your money, and don't go crazy spending every dollar you make on liabilities, then you will be sure to obtain financial freedom. Stay disciplined on your path to financial freedom. Let's stop living rich and dying broke.

Financial Rule #5: Credit...that's how they did it.

You have two types of people in this world: those who know how to use credit to their advantage, and those who abuse their credit. Unfortunately, the public school system doesn't have this in their curriculum. Young boys and girls should be taught the importance of credit.

Credit, in my opinion, is the most powerful tool you have, yes, even more powerful than money. An 800 credit score has more purchasing power than $100,000. That's not just my opinion, but that's what I've also learned from the wealthy. I know that may sound odd, because if you were taught like me, then you were taught that debt is bad, and we should stay away from it.

That is true, but I'll add by saying that not all debt is bad debt. Have you ever wondered how the wealthy actually gained their wealth? Or as Jay-Z best put it, "You want to know what's more important than throwing away money at a strip club? Credit. Do you ever wonder why Jewish people own all the property in America? Well, this is how they did it." You see, there is "good debt." It takes money to make money, and that's where constructive debt comes into play. If you could borrow money for 6% interest annually and invest the money in assets that would pay you 10% or more annually, would you agree that this kind of debt could eventually make you wealthy?

If you borrow money from the bank, the loan is a liability, but if you take that money and invest it into something that pays you much more than you are paying the bank, whatever you invest in is an asset, and the bank loan becomes constructive debt. Don't borrow money unless you can put it to work and have it earn more than it costs you to borrow it.

The wealthy understands how to leverage debt to build their wealth. How do you think Grant Cardone or Sam Zell got his hands on some of the biggest apartment complexes? Credit, that's how he did it! Jerry Jones bought the Dallas Cowboys and the stadium for $140 million in 1989. He put up $90 million in cash and financed the rest using his...CREDIT. He went all in on that purchase, and many critics ridiculed him on the purchase. Donald Trump even passed up on the deal five years earlier and had an opportunity to buy the team for $50 million. Today, the Dallas Cowboys are worth $5 billion, so I'd say Jerry Jones' risk paid off big time!

Like money, if you don't use credit wisely, then you will suffer the consequences. People take out credit lines every day. Students take out student loans. Consumers are getting new credit cards. People are taking out personal loans to catch up on bills. People are taking out auto loans to buy cars. People are taking our mortgage loans to buy houses. These are just some of biggest areas of credit usage in America.

What's in your wallet? Capital One has built their company using that one question in their marketing. They have built their company by issuing credit cards to consumers like you and me. They want us to have one of their cards in our wallets. Why are they giving out so many lines of credits to millions of people? They make billions in interest charges every year from the millions of Americans who have their cards. According to an article written by Alexandre Tanzi at Bloomberg, U.S. credit card debt closed 2018 at a record $870 billion. That's the largest credit debt ever.

When I first got credit cards, I wasn't using them properly. I went on a shopping frenzy with those cards from buying video games, buying $100 pair of jeans, and just flat out buying liabilities. At first, I literally thought it was "free money." That's just how naïve I was about credit. When I began to understand how credit works, like so many of us, I developed the mentality of, "Oh, I can just pay this later." Well, "later" turned into maxed out credit cards; maxed out credit cards turned into late payments; late payments turned into no payments; no payments turned into delinquencies; delinquencies turned into closed out cards; closed out cards with unpaid balances led to having a negative impact on my credit. At one point, my credit had dropped to as low as 450!

If I would have known then what I know now, I would have used my credit more wisely. The good news is that I was young when I made those mistakes, and I was young when I corrected my mentality and those mistakes. Remember, I'm still in my 20s right now. That goes back to what I was saying last chapter: time is your most valuable asset. The younger you make mistakes, the younger you can correct those mistakes. You never fail in life. You either win or you learn (which then results in winning).

Here's what I now know about credit. In order to build and maintain great credit, you must avoid:

- **Making late payments.**
- **Carrying big balances (keep your credit usage 30% or below. Keep it 10% or below if you really want to boost your credit score).**
- **Closing a credit line for no reason (you need a good lengthy credit history).**
- **Having too many credit inquires. If you are shopping for a car or house within 45 days, all of those inquiries will count as one).**
- **Defaulting on loans or credit cards!**

Credit is extremely important. I'll say once again, in my opinion, it's even more powerful than cash. If you want to build wealth and obtain freedom in your life, you must absolutely learn how to use your credit strategically. Credit is a crucial piece to the financial game.

Financial Rule #6: Stop working for the money. Invest and get free.

Again, as my great friend James Setzer posted to our Real Men Empowerment group on Facebook, "I challenge you all to think out of the box! You don't have to abide by the traditional methods of life. Do you want to be the guy busting your butt all year for a $1.00 raise? Or do you want to save money and invest in a side hustle that will give you extra cash flow. What could you do with an extra $2,000 a month in cash? $3,000? $5,000? There's a cap on how much you earn at a job, no matter how much work you put in, but there is no cap for the cash flow you can produce by simply putting your money to work."

Do you ever dream of living life on your own terms; you know, wake up when you want to, go to bed when you want to, travel when you want to, and stop having to clock in at that job that you hate? Have you ever just wanted to live life and not worry if this bill or that bill is going to get paid? Have you ever just wanted to live a decent stress-free life? Have you ever wanted to just be free? Well, as one of my mentors once told me, "If you want a life where you are free, stop working for the money, and put that money to work for you." I replied, "What do you mean by stop working for the money?" Well, let me share with you what I learned.

There are 3 types of ways you can receive income: earned, portfolio, and passive. Earned income is income that is a direct result of your labor, or trading your time for money (i.e. clocking in at your job). Portfolio income is money received from investments, dividends, interest, and capital gains (i.e. stocks, bonds, art, etc.). Passive income is a revenue stream that may require some initial effort or expenditure, but doesn't require any day-to-day labor or require you to be "hands on," and continues to reap payments down the line for as long as you own that asset (i.e. music and book royalties, rental property, etc.).

In order to obtain a life of freedom, you must eventually replace your earned income for passive income. In other words, stop being a slave to the clock and get into position to get off that clock. Stop working for the money, and make that money work for you.

"So, how do I create passive income, Mr. Janders?" I'm glad you asked.

You create passive income by investing. There are multiple things that you could invest in that could create passive income for you, but for example purposes, I'll share one of my favorite investment vehicles and something that has created 90% of the world's millionaires: real estate.

If you discipline yourself to save money and take care of your credit, then you can get yourself into position to purchase some real estate, more specifically rental property. There are many different types of rental properties: apartment complexes, strip malls, single family homes, duplexes, triplexes, fourplexes, etc.

Let's say that you work at BMW making $30 an hour, and you want to start creating passive income so that you can eventually get off BMW's clock. You put yourself on a strict budget and start saving every dollar that you can, even your bonuses. While you are saving, you start reading books on rental property investing so that you educate yourself and gain more understanding about rental investing.

Fast forward, your money is now saved up pretty good, and your credit is excellent, so you start searching for your first rental property. You find a triplex that's listed for $190,000. You purchase the property, and let's say your mortgage is

$1000 a month. You live in one door while you are renting the other two doors out for $1000. This gives you the ability to "live free" because one door is paying your mortgage for you while the other door could be giving you positive cash flow.

After a while of "house hacking," you sell that property so that you could buy a larger property. You find a 32-unit apartment complex and hire a property manager to oversee the day-to-day operations of the property while you sit back and collect your monthly dividends from your investment. Now you are truly collecting passive income and living a life of freedom to enjoy with your family however you please.

This is just one of many ways that you could "put your money to work" and create passive income. The key is to not just save money—because money sitting in an account or under a mattress doesn't do anything for you—but to invest money. DO have an emergency savings in place for life's curveballs as I discussed in rule number 3, but aside from that, invest, invest, invest.

Rapper Offset shared in his Breakfast Club interview about how he became "financially woke." He says $260,000 of where he lives (which is Atlanta, GA) can get you some nice condos to buy and rent out. He's a rapper, so it's very easy for him to get caught up in the hype of just buying liabilities, but instead, he said, "I can buy condos for that much money. Let me get five of those condos, because they don't depreciate like cars do." He also spoke about buying apartment complexes in Atlanta with his wife Cardi B!

The wealthy are wealthy because they invest their money and create multiple streams of income. They live a life of financial freedom by creating passive income for themselves. The goal is to save and invest in hard assets that produce income, and keep doing that until your passive income is greater than your earned income. I heard once that being rich is having money, but being wealthy is having time. If you keep the "work for the money" mentality, then you will never be free and in control of this financial game. Creating passive income can alleviate any financial stress that would come with economic downturns in life.

These are the 6 rules that have helped me elevate and continue to help me elevate financially. My goal here is to give you another way to view finances. You and I weren't just born to pay bills and die. We weren't born to just survive. We were born to live life in abundance. By educating ourselves financially (rule #1), changing our relationship with our finances (rule #2), being in control of our finances (rule #3), living modestly (rule #4), taking care of our credit (rule #5), and putting our money to work (rule #6), only then will we see our finances and life elevate.

5 Money traps to avoid

1. Buying a home or renting an apartment that's too expensive should be avoided. And if you really want to build wealth, you may even want to consider teaming up and living with some friends or family. You guys can live together, cut expenses, and invest and build your money up together. Just take a look at the Hispanics, Koreans, or Chinese for example. This helped me and my family big time!

2. Going on vacations that you can't afford. I made this mistake once because I wanted to "live life," and it ended up costing me in the long run. Spending about eight grand in Miami, just to come back and play catch up is not good at all. That was a big mistake.

3. Buying or leasing a car that's out of your price range. Can you afford that 2020 Mercedes Benz?

4. Accumulating massive debt. Remember credit—like cash—can be your best friend or your worst enemy, depending on how you use it.

5. Marrying and/or having a baby with the wrong person. This is the biggest one in my opinion. Marriages can get very expensive if it's with the wrong person, especially when divorce comes into the picture. Likewise, don't let your sexual impulse have you making a decision that could cost you down the road. Don't let 30 minutes of temporary satisfaction lead you to a lifelong mistake of making a baby with the wrong person. The mistake is not the baby itself of course, but the mistake can be with whom you have a baby with. Whenever you have sex with someone, you are taking a 50/50 chance at having a baby. Nothing on the market is 100% preventive, so if you know you are not ready to become a parent or deal with any baby mother/father drama, then choose your partner wisely. How many people do you know that claim having a baby with the mother or father of their child was a mistake? Marriage is 80% business and 20% love. We'll go more in depth with this in chapter 8.

5 Reasons why people spend money they don't have

1. **Peer pressure**. Pressuring yourself to keep up with those around you will often have you spending money that you don't have. Fear of missing out on a good time; I can't even count the times that I've done this in the past. I used to live for the summertime trips and weekends, only to come back home being more broke than before I left. Don't let the *fear* of missing out on a good time make you spend money that you don't have.

2. **Impressing someone their dating**. When you first start dating someone, it can be very tempting to "go all out" on your partner all the time. It can be tempting to go to the most expensive restaurants on every date or to go to the most expensive mall. You don't have to go big for your partner every time. Only do what you can afford.

3. **Depression**. Believe it or not, people tend to spend money more when they are depressed, because whatever their purchasing is a temporary band aid to make them feel better. Be careful of this if this is you.

4. **Holidays and Birthdays.** Holidays and birthdays eat our pockets big time every year. Many of us literally go into debt around holidays. You think you are getting deals on "Black Friday," but are you? We use "Christmas spirit" as an excuse for us to blow thousands of dollars that we don't have. Of course, you love your children, but is buying them a lot of crap they are not going to

care about 20 years from now going to help them? My daughters live in the same household with me, so I can buy them gifts any time. I'm married to my wife, so I can take her on a nice date or book a getaway anytime, so what is a valentine's day? All the money you spend on holidays and birthdays can be used to build wealth for you and your family. Buy your children some bonds instead of toys that you are going to be selling for pennies at a yard sale. Build a business that you could pass along. I'm not saying don't celebrate holidays and birthdays. I'm saying just don't go overboard on the holidays with money you don't have. Don't force yourself.

5. **"The stack all winter, spend all summer" mentality.** This reason alone is why many of us don't make any progress financially. We work overtime all winter at our jobs and stack up money for the summer, and when the summer comes, we blow it all on trips, parties, outfits, etc. We repeat the cycle the very next winter. "Work all winter, spend it all in the summer" is a vicious cycle that we must break. Again, I'm not saying that we can't have fun in the summer, but if you want to build wealth, you are going to have to sacrifice a few summers, sacrifice a few trips, and sacrifice a few parties. The wealthy people you see traveling and enjoying life now weren't doing those things when they were my age at 27. They were locked in on building their business or their investments, and that required them to show up in the summertime too; not just the winter.

Conclusion

Again, money is not the root of all evil. Money isn't the problem; it's what some people do in pursuit of money or do with money after they get it that causes problems. Money is not the root of all evil; it's just a tool, a common means of exchange.

For banks, money is their inventory, just as shoes are to a shoe store. They buy money wholesale (what they pay depositors) and sell it at retail (the interest they charge on loans).

Lack of money will create other problems in your life that you don't want. With money, you will experience less stress knowing that your bills are paid on time. How good would it be to give your body the proper care that it needs? How good would it be to be able to afford a healthy diet rather than to settle for McDonald's dollar menu? How good would it be to travel and experience the world rather than to look at the same ole streets in the town in which you grew up? How good would it be to still live comfortably through a recession or when a pandemic like the Coronavirus hit the country like it did in early 2020?

Having one source of income is dangerous. I don't care how much money you make, if it's only coming from one source, it's a problem. That's why we must create a road map for our money. We must stop living for the "right now" and live for the future. We have to break this poverty cycle.

The wealthy are no different than you and I. If they can put their pants on the same way that we put ours on and build wealth, so can you and I. There are so many more important things in the world than money, so get your money up so you can focus on them, not having to focus on being limited due to lack of money.

"Change the way you view money, and your relationship with money will change. If you have a broke mindset, then your bank account will always be broke; even if you make $30 an hour."

Ask yourself the following:
- What's holding me back from financial freedom?
- How can I gain more education that can help me elevate financially?
- Who can I learn from?
- What do I stress about the most?
- Am I in control of my finances right now?

CHAPTER 7

Guilty By Association

"If you look at the people in your circle and don't get inspired, then you don't have a circle, you have a cage."- Nipsey Hussle

If you come into my home (my kingdom), you will see pictures of lions posted throughout my home. Look on my social media and you see how much I post lions. I fell in love with lions at the age of 4 when I first watched *The Lion King* (more on that in chapter 10). My love and passion for lions is actually how I came up with the cover, my everyday motto, and the title of this book, *Success Is My Prey*.

There is no secret that lions hunt and eat what they kill. It's also no secret that when they hunt for prey, they tend to hunt with fellow lions and lionesses that are in their pride, especially prey that's five times their size. They understand that their strength is in numbers. Knowing that about lions helped me realize that I needed to be aware of who I surround myself with if I wanted to elevate and obtain great success in life.

You've probably heard it before, but there's a saying that goes something like, "show me five of your friends, and I'll show you your future." When I first came across that quote, it forced me to really evaluate my inner circle of influence. I had thoughts that lead to questions like, What kind of energy am I exposing myself to? Are the people around me trying to elevate in life? What are we doing with our time together?

After thinking about those questions, I realized that part of what was holding me back from elevating my life was the dead weight that was weighing me down, and I knew that I had to make a change. I needed lions around me that wanted to elevate and eat like me.

I'm sure you've probably heard of the world-renowned boxer, and in my opinion, the GOAT (greatest of all time), Muhammed Ali. Ali may have been named one of the greatest boxing champions that have ever stepped into a ring, but without the individuals around him, he would have never been that great boxer. From his boxing coach Angelo Dundee; his trainer and speechwriter Drew Bundini Brown; his ringside physician Ferdie Pacheco; to his corner man Jabir Herbert Muhammed and many others, Ali had a team of individuals contributing to his success. And the more success he gained, the more success THEY gained.

A team is made up of individuals that share the same vision and come together for the same goals. As with any sport, you are only as good as the people on your team. The same holds true for life. You are only as good in life as the people you associate yourself with personally and professionally.

Your Personal Association

Personally, I know a lot of people. I used to have a lot of friends, or at least thought I needed a lot of friends. I was (and still am) a social butterfly. I just love people! But when I read the quote, "Show me five of your friends, and I'll show you your future," I realized my future was dependent on the company and energy I kept around me. When I finally "opened my eyes," I realized I was allowing too many toxic relationships from family and friends to have a negative impact on me. I was smoking, drinking, clubbing, chasing females, and engaging in illegal activities with those people.

To be honest, I knew deep down inside that lifestyle wasn't truly who I was. I was forcing myself into what I thought was "cool." I knew I had to move on from them, because whenever I would bring up positive things or wanting better out of life, they would just laugh and clown me. They would tell me I was being lame. One those old friends even wanted to fight me because I was trying to change for the better!

I tried to bring those guys along the journey, but the truth is, I had outgrown those guys. That is also when I realized that sometimes we just outgrow certain people. Don't try to fix it; just accept it and move forward with your life.

Today, my personal association is relatively small, but yet, much more powerful compared to my former association. My association is my household family, my positive outside family, and my friends who are just like family. These people help lift me up, and I also lift them up.

Once I changed my energy to be more positive, I started to attract positive individuals into my life. Ever since these positive individuals have appeared, my life has certainly elevated to higher levels. We help push and support each other in our marriages, parenthood, manhood, businesses, jobs, etc. I love my entire family (blood and friends who are family), and I couldn't ask for a better support system.

The best relationships happen organically, and are not forced. You don't ask anyone, "Do you want to be my friend?" Energy and vibrations are real, so you naturally attract the energy that you put out. Be aware of those who are in your life and make sure they are adding value into your life. Make sure you are also adding value into their lives. Your personal association will have the greatest impact on your life, as this circle will most likely consist of close family members, close friends, and even those who you enter a romantic relationship with. Like your finances, you want assets, not liabilities.

Goal Blooded Hunters

"Don't mix business with pleasure" has been another saying that's been around for a while. It's basically saying don't mix personal relationships with business, and don't allow business relationships to get too personal. Leave work associates at work. This is true for the most part. Just because someone is your friend or family, doesn't mean they are right for you as a business partner, and vice versa.

In some cases, however, you can have a professional relationship with family or friends, if, and only if, you guys are on the same page. In my opinion, a lot of people fail to carefully separate their personal and professional associations. I know I did in the past as well.

When I first started my investment group, and when I wanted to start doing some big investing, I wanted to bring my close friends and family along the journey. I had a clear vision, and I wanted them to be able to come along to build and do some investing with me. I even had two separate family meetings where I laid out plans of action.

I quickly found out, however, that it wasn't going to work. You can't force family into investing and doing business together, especially when they don't want what you want out of life (The one person who is on my business team and we are 50/50 partners is, of course, my wonderful wife).

Forcing business with close family and friends just because I had relationships with them turned out to be a costly mistake. It definitely affected my wife and me. Once the plan(s) didn't go through, I went back to my whiteboard and hit the reset button on my business plans. During one of my meditating moments, I reflected and thought to myself, *don't try to force people to come onboard. The right people will come when they come. Even if it's just you and your wife, the vision will come to reality.* Once I fully accepted that, the journey to building really started taking place.

I started attending business seminars, networking events, and even used my social media to build professional relationships with people outside of my personal association.

I started seeking mentorship from people who also owned their own business as well. I started seeking partnerships with people who actually wanted to win in business and in life. I needed goal blooded hunters around me who would be ready to risk, grind, and fight for the *prey*.

From Beating The "Trap"...

As I told you earlier, I grew up in the "hood" or "the projects."; a.k.a the Section 8 low-income housing authority for the most part of my life. I grew up seeing and experiencing things that I think no child should have to witness. I saw a lot of my peers sell drugs, and I saw a lot of my peers do drugs, even in my very own family. I heard gun shots so much that they didn't faze me anymore, and I was sleeping right through them at night. I would just hear a story at the bus stop the next morning about who got shot or whose house got shot up the night before. I saw the police take someone to jail almost every day.

Not many black people get to make it out of those environments without being added to the prison or death statistics. A lot of my peers that I grew up with and older people from those neighborhoods are either in prison or six feet under right now. I barely made it out without getting killed, but not before I would get that Strong-Armed Robbery charge at 17. I didn't make it in the death statistics, but I certainly made the convicted felon statistics.

I became a part of a system that my mom tried to warn me about. I grew up a nice young man, played sports, and took care of my younger siblings. Then one day I found myself smoking, drinking, carrying brass knuckles and a pistol. Like many of my peers, the environment had gotten the best of me, and I soon fell into the street life that they were a part of.

That negative environment has left a lot of people mentally paralyzed. A lot of people that I know from back then have stopped trying to elevate their life, or they never started because of their mental limitation and the mental "trapping" effect that environment played.

After experiencing jail and seeing my life flash before my eyes, I became very adamant on creating a better environment for myself. I knew that there was a better world out there than what I was witnessing every day. I knew that it was a better life, and most importantly, I knew that I wanted to have children someday and didn't want my children to have to experience that type of environment. I knew once I changed the condition of my mind, then my outside conditions would naturally change for the better.

...To Multimillion Dollar Environments

Have you ever had a conversation with a multimillionaire? Because I grew up in such a dark place, I used to be envious of the wealthy and the middle class. I used to think that it was unfair for them to live such a good life, and that those of us in the poor class couldn't. I was envious of the kids in the suburbs because they had everything that I wanted in life. They had two-parent homes, they had a decent house, they got to travel a lot, they had nice meals; I just felt like they had it better, and

I was angry because I couldn't experience the same thing. As I got older, my perspective changed, and I thought to myself, *why be mad when you can learn from these people?*

Visiting my aunt Daaliyah during Summer and Spring breaks gave me more motivation to elevate for sure. Her and her husband at the time provided an escape from the reality that I was faced with every day. They lived the life that I wished I had. They were in a nice suburban neighborhood, two-parent home, took nice trips, and their children seemed to not want for much. My siblings and I thought they were millionaires for sure. It's because of my aunt and her husband why I'm an avid reader today, and study wealth the way that I do. They were leading the way to show my generation that it is possible to elevate in life, and your circumstances can change if you work to make it happen.

So I started studying the wealthy or those that had what seemed to be a better life than me. I wanted to learn what they knew. I wanted to learn their success as well as their mistakes. I started reading books and tried talking with local wealthy individuals. One thing that I noticed as I started studying these people is that the majority of them started with humble beginnings just as I did. Some would open up, and some wouldn't, but the point is that I started placing myself in environments where I could directly and indirectly learn from those who were in better positions than I was, especially with finances and business.

I started putting myself in environments where I knew people with influence would be. I spend time in upscale venues that attract these people. I love playing golf now. When I travel out of town, I don't get Motel 6. To be clear, it's not because I think I'm too good for a Motel 6 or that something is wrong with a cheap motel, but it's more about positioning myself to network with people who have businesses and wealth. The conversations are just different, and I'm all for it.

Besides, I've experienced the bottom of life and know how that feels, so now I want to experience the better things in life. I used to have to make pallets on floors and sleep in homeless shelters; so what's wrong with getting on yachts and enjoying a nice view of Downtown Miami from the top floor of the balcony at the beautiful Epic Miami Hotel?

Don't Be Afraid To Change up

There are 3 things that I've learned along my journey:
1. Everybody won't understand your vision, but keep going anyway.
2. Life is like a bus ride. People may get on your bus, but they'll get off at their destination.
3. It took me a while to grasp this, but YOU CAN'T TAKE EVERYBODY WITH YOU. When they do depart, hold grudges, or harbor feelings, they were only doing what was designed for them to do.

Guilty by association is who or what you surround yourself with. If you surround yourself with negative individuals and/ or hang around negative environments, you will be exposed to negative opportunities that will increase your chances of making negative choices. If you are in the car with someone who has drugs on them, you will also get charged with the drugs, even if they aren't yours and you are "innocent." That's guilty by negative association, my friend.

If you surround yourself with positive individuals and/ or hang around positive environments, you will be exposed to positive opportunities that will increase your chances of making more positive life choices. If you friend is elevating, and you are elevating, then that's guilty by positive association.

Negative people and negative environments are only roadblocks on your path to success. Negative people in your life are too expensive. What I mean by that is, if you don't cut ties with negative people and negative environments, you will pay a huge price in the future. As I said before: you want assets in your life, not liabilities. This is the time where you start to discover who your true friends and family are.

Sometimes the weight you need to lose isn't on your body. Rid yourself of any dead weight around you. Associate yourself with others who encourage you to win. Sometimes you just outgrow certain people, including close childhood family and friends. Just accept reality for what it is and move forward.

When I was hanging with "the wrong crowd" and being in the wrong environments, I was definitely living the wrong life. Ever since I shifted towards the positive crowds and positive environments, I have been living my absolute best life. I stopped hanging with friends who were spending money and started hanging with friends who wanted to make money together.

I read this statement once, "The less you associate with some people, the more your life will improve. Any time you tolerate mediocrity in others, it increases your mediocrity. An important attribute in successful people is their impatience with negative thinking and negative acting people."

As you grow on your journey, your associates will change. That's natural. Don't be afraid of the change that will come. People who you grew up with will say negative things about the person you will become, because they still remember you for who you were, and not who you are becoming. But as Jay-Z said once in an interview, "People will look at you and say you changed, like you worked that hard to stay the same."

Some of your childhood friends and family will not want you to go on. They will want you to stay where they are mentally, physically, spiritually, and financially. If they don't help you climb, they will indeed help you crawl. Your friends will help stretch your vision or choke your dreams and ambitions. Those that don't increase you will eventually decrease you.

No one in history ever did it alone when it comes to elevating in life. It takes a solid team to accomplish bigger and better things in life. It takes the right association. History, however, tends to focus on the individual, and not the collective. No matter how *successful* someone's name or business may be, just know they didn't achieve or reach high levels all alone. They had/have the right association around them that you may not see behind the scenes.

Jay-Z wouldn't be who he is without his team. Kevin Hart gives credit to his team. Tom Brady may have six super bowl rings, and is arguably the best quarterback of all time, but he wouldn't be *"Tom Brady"* without his teammates and coaches positioning him for success. Michael Jordan is considered by many as the GOAT (Greatest Of All Time) of basketball, but it was his teammates and coaches around him that helped him win six championships in a row and dominate the league in the 1990s.

The only people I want around me are individuals who will stay on my head about not being where I have the potential to be. The people around me now hold me accountable and will legit confront me when I am slacking or not living up to my potential, and I absolutely love it.

You pick your surroundings, not the other way around. You should want to associate yourself with people who are going somewhere, who are focused and determined, and who are doing positive things in life. You can't afford to allow anyone to pull you down. Your success in life relies heavily on who you associate with. Remember, lions can certainly hunt their own prey, but with the right association around, they can take down bigger prey together.

#SuccessIsMyPreyChallenge: I challenge you to position yourself around people and environments that challenge you to grow. Don't be intimidated by those who may be in a better position than you. That is your opportunity to learn, grow, and build with solid individuals in positive driven environments. Be very selective with who you associate yourself with. Don't worry about having a lot of friends. Just focus on having solid relationships in your life.

Chapter 8

What's Love Got To Do With It?

"Love can either make you or break you in life, depending on who you're dealing with."- J.ANDERS

Two of the most important decisions that you will make in your life is who you marry and who you have children with. These two decisions have helped a lot of people, but I've also seen these very same two decisions hurt a lot of people. What I'm going to share with you in this chapter is very critical to your success journey. I'm talking about the significance of our romantic lives and understanding who we choose as our partners in life. It doesn't matter if you're single, currently in a relationship right now, or looking for your next relationship.

I mentioned last chapter that no one has ever achieved a high level of success truly by themselves. There's a quote that says, "Behind every successful man, there's a strong woman."

That quote may be talking about a man, but it is equally true for women as well. I would say behind every successful man or woman is a strong partner/mate who helped them elevate. Your partner in life will directly impact how much you achieve in your life.

When I talk about my wife to anyone, I just sum the conversation up in two words: lucky and blessed. When I first met my wife, I just knew she was the one. She was a strong, determined, and ambitious young woman; and I was a strong, determined, and ambitious young man. We both knew we wanted our future lives individually and our future relationships to be better than our past. I already wanted to elevate personally in my life, and she wanted to elevate in her life, so when we actually became *one*, our elevation really went to another level.

We share the same morals in life, and vision for our family. We have joined our worlds together and have learned so much from one another. She has taught me about the natural side of life, from foods to natural medicine, and I have taught her about business, investing, and entrepreneurship. Together we have become more financially savvy, and together we have learned more about our spirituality.

She graduated high school with a 4.9 GPA, and when we met, she was just transferring to Clemson University. As for me, I was a GED grad, on felony probation, and was just starting at a community college. At first, I didn't tell her about my past, or about me being recently convicted of a felony because I thought I would scare her off. I thought she was out of my league. To my surprise, I was wrong. Even though she seemed to be a little more advanced than I was, she still saw potential in me. She didn't judge who I was based off of my past. She liked who I was at that moment, and she saw the potential in who I was trying to become.

Throughout the course of our eight-year marriage, she has been a true rider, and a solid partner to do life with. When we first moved together and didn't have much money, we both slept on a twin mattress. The first ring I bought her was a big fake ring online. When I first started talking about building my own clothing brand, she was saving all of the checks from her job so that she could help invest (she's actually the one who named our company).

Another thing I love about her is that she has the ability to see things before I can see things sometimes. She has helped prevent me from making some costly mistakes, but she also has helped me through some costly decisions. She loved me at times when I was being selfish and didn't deserve her love. We have enjoyed ourselves in places like Miami, but we have also been down to our lowest to the point if it wasn't for family helping us, we would have otherwise been out on the streets homeless, due to poor decisions and lack of discipline on my end.

Most women would have walked away from some of the things that we've been through, and from some of my weak periods, but she chose to stay and still pushes me to be a better man because she knows how great I can be. I push her to be great, and she pushes me to be even greater. She wants to see me win just as bad as I want to see her win. She has my last name and we are a team. We are for each other, and not against each other.

She takes very good care of the home with her stay-at-home mom role, and she's one heck of a mother to our girls. I'm also blessed that not only is she my wife, but she is the mother of our beautiful daughter Ashyra. We waited five and a half years into our marriage to have our first baby.

It was just my wife and I for the longest, and we both had good paying jobs, low expenses, and no other responsibilities other than a dog we had. So we were spending unnecessary money on trips and outings with friends and family. We were going out to eat at nice restaurants all the time. As I said last chapter, there is nothing wrong with enjoying the finer things in life, but it is careless to blow money and not capitalize on the opportunity to set up for the future.

When I found out that I was becoming a father for the first time, and as most first-time parents, I was both excited and nervous. I was excited because I was having my first child, but I was nervous because I knew there was going to be another life, another human depending on me to lead and guide her through life. I was scared because I felt as if I wasn't ready to take on that role just yet.

I mainly got nervous because I felt that we weren't in the financial position that I wanted us to be in prior to having kids. Honestly, with all the money my wife and I had flowing in, we had no excuse not to be in a great financial position, but because of our poor choices, lack of financial knowledge, and MY lack of discipline, we found ourselves behind financially or just flat out broke to put it simply. Things really got rough when my wife was forced to stop working in the middle of the pregnancy, and we were knocked down to just one income.

When my wife went out of work, and with about four months left until our daughter was born, I really turned up the grind on my first business venture. I launched THE J.ANDERS BRAND™, but it wasn't exactly the release that I wanted. It was more of an urgent "I need to create extra money!" type of launch. I did pretty well in the first few months of business, but with no true system in place for the business, things took a downward dive. Because I had no system in place, and I was doing everything at a fast panicking pace, I wasn't putting my best foot forward with the quality of my products, because I was just so focused on making money.

During the four months before our daughter was born, my wife and I had to move out of our townhome, and we even had to separate for about two months so that I could stay closer to my job while she went with her people who lived about an hour away. I was working twelve hour shifts at my day job and preparing orders for shipment at night in the garage of my mom's house. I wasn't really sleeping at all.

Although I was urgently trying to create extra money, I was putting my body and our little family through so much, because of the mistake of not carefully planning for our child, our finances, and this new found business venture as well.

Every day, living apart from my wife became more and more challenging. I was trying to smile and fight my way through it, but the pressure was definitely getting to me. My wife needed me with her more than anything. She was becoming more stressed throughout the pregnancy. So, with about a month left before our daughter was born, I was faced with a big-time decision. I either had to stay where I was and keep trying to force this business out the panic state that I was in, or move about an hour and half away from my job in order to be with my wife.

I decided to move so that I could be back with my wife. It was at that moment when I realized that my wife and unborn daughter needed me more than anything. I figured that I can always build a business, but I can't afford to put my family on the back burner, just for the sake of building a business and making money. In addition to that, I also realized that it doesn't make much sense to try and build another business when I can't even run my current personal business effectively (my household). I definitely had to be there for her.

My mentor and financial advisor told me once, "Jared, always listen to your wife." Yes, I wanted to work on the business, but I had to listen to my wife when she cried out for me to be by her side. I decided that we would worry about building our business later, but at that point, we had to focus on getting back to us and building our foundation back strong.

Every relationship will have "rock bottom seasons" at various points in the relationship, and our first rock bottom season definitely hit us in 2017. Financial hard times with constant over drafted accounts, both of our credit scores dropping tremendously, a newborn on the way, and trying to create our first business that year, caused us to have major stress in our lives. We eventually created a game plan, got disciplined and extremely focused, and turned things around.

Yes, we made some big mistakes together, but as I said about myself earlier, we were fortunate to be young enough to make them and young enough to learn from those mistakes.

If we don't have anything else, we know we have each other. I have her back and she has mine. Despite our rock bottom season, we still had strong belief that our future was going to be incredible. We made promises to each other to not repeat the same mistakes. We knew there were opportunities for us both to get better, and we wanted to get better. We knew the opportunity to gain financial freedom was there, and we didn't have to settle for poverty and bring our children through it just like we did. We wanted to correct those mistakes and turn those losses into lessons. We both knew we wanted generational wealth and positive generational trends to leave behind for our family.

That rock bottom experience with my wife taught me the importance of planning and getting prepared for whatever it is I will do in life. I should have already started my business and carefully planned it out so that I would put out great quality products. I should have already been prepared for a child financially, so that I wouldn't have to be forced to rush into that business venture. Most importantly, I should have planned for the unknown in life.

We didn't know my wife was going to be at risk and would have to stop working earlier than expected. I can go on about I should have, could have, and would have, but in the end, the mistakes were made, and I have since learned from and corrected those mistakes by now carefully planning and analyzing events in my life before they take place.

The Most Powerful Piece In The Game

You may or may not be familiar with the game of chess, but what is the most powerful piece on the chess board? What piece can move freely and anywhere on the board? What piece sits beside the king and aids as an important protection for the king? That's right, the queen! The queen is the most powerful piece on the chess board. She can move in ways that a king can't.

My wife is the most powerful person on my team and in my life. She directs me and helps me get better as a king every day. She's helping me hustle towards our goal of financial freedom. I lean heavy on her advice as she helps me with making decisions. She's the organizer behind the scenes while I'm the executer out in front. You may see my face a lot on social media, on billboards, or wherever, but you better believe that without my wife, I wouldn't be where I am today. She's the ultimate driving force behind me.

The True 80/20 Rule

In chapter 6, I said that marriage is 80% business and 20% love. Let's take a deeper look at what I meant by that. The 80/20 rule for my wife and I is different from most people's 80/20 rule. We believe that marriage/relationships are 80% business and 20% love. Actor and former NFL player Devale Ellis broke this down perfectly in an Instagram post, and I couldn't have said it any better, so I'll share his words right here:

"The 80/20 rule means something completely different to me. To me marriage is 80% business and 20% love. After years of

following my heart and feeling lost, I learned to follow my head and found the way to build our love story.

Most relationships don't fail because of infidelity—they fail because of resentment and stress caused by financial pressures that can ultimately lead to infidelity. As millennials, our ideas of marriage don't necessarily match the socioeconomic conditions we are facing as adults. Not having financial security leads to insecurities that manifest themselves in other areas of our relationships.

I noticed very early how finances affected our intimacy— which affected our ability to parent effectively. So I stopped making short-term decisions for a quick smile of gratitude from the woman I loved, and started making long- term sacrifices that garnished a permanent smile of trust from the teammate I will be building with for the rest of my life. As a man, this sent my confidence through the roof and ultimately spiked our intimacy. This idea that I could create the life I want with the woman I want became a reality…and it started the day I stopped looking

at marriage through the lens of a naïve child that grew up watching Disney movies and rap videos. It happened when I started viewing marriage as a business, as opposed to a fairy tale where things just magically happen on its own. IF IT WAS GOING TO WORK, I HAD TO MAKE IT WORK. DEAD ASS!"

I couldn't have said what Devale said any better. Marriage is business. Family is business. The quicker we understand that, the quicker we will stop wasting time in our love lives.

On the song "Show Me Love (remix)," music artist 21 Savage said, "And money ain't nothing, there's people who **happy** in love, and they behind on they bills, and they haven't paid they mortgage in years." Although it sounded nice in the song, I can't totally agree with what he said. I can't fathom the thought of being in love but struggling and being stressed out financially. My wife and I decided that we weren't going to live that way either. If we were to be in love, then we wanted to be spending our love life enjoying each other as stress free as possible. How many couples do you know that are "in love" but settle for a life filled with struggling and liabilities?

Your partner should be an asset and bring value to your life, if not, then he or she is a liability in your life. I don't care how much you love someone, a liability is a liability. If you meet someone and all they want to do is "live life and spend money" on liabilities while you're trying to build wealth and obtain financial freedom, then that should be a sign to drop him or her from your life. If your partner can't make sacrifices with you for a vision to make you guys' future better, then they should be dropped from your life. If your partner isn't hustling and building right beside you, then they are in the way.

I always found it funny when people used to ask where my wife worked, and I would reply that she worked at home. They would then reply with "what does she do at home?" I would then reply, "She's a stay-at-home wife/mom, and she helps me run a business that we own together." After hearing that, some women would be quick to say things like, "See, I need a man who's going to take care of me. I need an athlete or a man with some money. I'm tired of working; I'm ready to be a stay-at-home mom." They don't realize how silly they sound when they start talking like that.

The point that they miss is that my wife isn't "just a stay- at-home mom who's just living off of her man's money." She's HELPING me build a solid future for OUR family. When I first met her, she was working at Walmart, and then Chick- fil-A while being a full-time student at Clemson University.

She worked at Greenville Memorial Hospital and saved her checks to help invest in OUR first business. Yes, she had to suddenly stop working in the middle of our first daughter's pregnancy, but once we bounced back from that setback, her staying at home became a BUSINESS decision that WE made together. The decision was made, not because she just wants to be home, lazy, and have her man take care of her like so many women want, but it was the best decision for our daughters and our family as a whole moving forward. Trust me; she knows how to take care of herself. She doesn't NEED me to take care of her.

For starters, a woman going back to work six weeks after pregnancy is just not fair to her and the baby. A woman needs way more time than that (about a year in our book) to fully recover from a pregnancy, and also when a baby is so young in the world, bonding is real. Secondly, we don't have to worry about a $200 weekly daycare expense, and our daughters constantly getting sick at a daycare which would mean more medical expenses.

My first born was (and my second daughter currently is) exclusively breastfed, and our oldest is very advanced for her age because of the activities at home. She is our very own doctor and health nutritionists, so she keeps our health on the right track by cooking healthy meals for us and making our herbal supplements for us. She sets the tone for the inside of our home. I won't bore you with too many more details about our business decision, but the point is this: she is not a "lazy stay-at-home wife/mom who just wants a man to take care of her" like so many women want. She is my HELP MATE, BUSINESS PARTNER, and a wonderful LIFE PARTNER.

To further support my point on why relationships are 80% business and 20% love, Will and Jada Smith said in an interview that they created what they call a "marriage business plan" early on in their relationship. Will says, "If you don't have a purpose for your relationship, if you don't have a place that you're going, something that you want to accomplish, something that you want to do, you can really get lost in the murk of the journey. There has to be a vision. Like, why are we together?"

"The tough part is when two independent visions need to come together as one," Jada says. She goes on to say, "I had my vision and he had his, so we had to join it. Once we started to see how the children were growing, and you know, Willow, Jaden, and Trey were becoming their own beings, we decided, 'okay, we want to make a family business. How do we incorporate all the talent that we have in this family?' So that's our vision—to create a place where dreams can come true as well."

You may see a lot of power couples and admire their relationships, but I can assure you that they both understood that who they chose to be with was a key part to their success. Without Jada Pinkett, there would be no Will Smith, and without Will, there would be no Jada. Without Michelle

Obama, there would be no Barack Obama, and without Barack, there would be no Michelle. There would be no Shawn "Jay-Z" Carter without Beyoncé, and no Beyoncé without Jay-Z.

There would be no Devale Ellis without Khadeen Ellis, and no Khadeen without Devale. There would be no Jay Morrison without Ernestine Morrison, and no Ernestine without Jay. Without Ashley Smith, it definitely would not be a Jared Smith, and without Jared, it would be no Ashley.

Each name that I named in the foregoing paragraphs were already on track to be successful in their own way, but they found someone special that came into their life and amplified what they were already trying to achieve. We are all true kings and queens, and therefore, when we enter into a relationship with someone, we should seek to become a powerhouse couple and move WITH power.

Conclusion

If you are a male reading this, I can't stress it enough; be careful not to just fall for a woman's nice body figure. She may be beautiful on the outside, but she may not compliment who you are and what you are trying to build in life. Think with the head that's on top of your shoulders. Remember, if she's not an asset, then she's a liability.

If you are a woman reading this; don't allow a man to fast talk you into a relationship or just fall for his athletic build. He may talk a good game and may workout in the gym six days a week, but he may not fit well into your life with what you're trying to accomplish. Remember, he has to add value to your life. He has to be able and willing to build with you. If not, then do not waste time with him if he's showing you that he's a liability.

Although I say don't settle for someone who's a liability, it's just as important to make sure that YOU are an asset to someone else. You need to make sure that you are adding value to someone else's life just as well as you want them to add value to yours. A relationship works both ways, so make sure you are working on being the best version of yourself so that you can be an asset to someone's life.

Marrying and/or having a baby with the wrong person can be very costly. Don't allow thirty minutes of temporary satisfaction lead you to a lifelong mistake. The mistake, of course, is not the baby itself because a baby is the biggest blessing you will have, but the mistake can be with whom you have a baby. Remember, when you have sex, you are taking a 50/50 chance at having a baby (nothing on the market is 100% preventive).

Choose your partner wisely, or it could cost you big time; just ask those who have went through nasty divorces and/or have co-parenting issues. How many people do you know that claims having a baby with the mother or father of their child was a mistake? How many people do you know have allowed "love" to keep them in a toxic situation for far too long? At some point we must make an executive decision to remove ourselves from a partnership that isn't working. You are the CEO of your life, remember?

Remember, marriages/relationships are 80% business, and 20% love. Why do you think most divorces have to go through court to get resolved? Because that "paper" the couple signed was a contract, so whoever pushes for the divorce is essentially "buying" the other person out of the contract agreement. Marriage, children, and even just living together are all business before anything else. You may be functioning off love only, and that may be blinding you to the level of individual you're intertwining with. Until you recognize that, you're going to keep failing, or not elevate as far as you'd like

The man or woman you choose to be your partner affects everything in your life; your mental health, your peace of mind, your happiness, how you get through tragedies, your success, your finances, how your children will be raised, and so much more. So again, I say, your love life has everything to do with your success journey. These are life decisions that you will live with for the rest of your life. I'm fortunate that my WIFE just happens to be the MOTHER of my children. Two decisions that I can live in peace with for the rest of my life.

Chapter 9

That Ship Starts With You

"Give a man a fish and you will feed him for a day. Teach a man to fish, and you will feed him for a lifetime. Show him how to buy the pond, and no one in his family will ever know struggle."- Unknown

"The marathon continues."- R.I.P. Nipsey Hussle

The Lion King

One of my all-time favorite movies is *The Lion King*. In 2019, when the motion picture version of *The Lion King* was released, I was there, front and center, to watch it with my wife and daughter. Ever since watching the animated version in the 1990s as a young boy, I have always been empowered by the life lessons that were in the movie. Watching it again as a father in 2019 inspired me even more. If I had to describe the movie in one word, it would be: Legacy.

Mufasa was preparing to pass down the kingdom (PrideRock) to his son Simba. He was teaching Simba key lessons and words that would be with him throughout life. He was preparing Simba to be the next reigning king. He was preparing to leave a legacy for Simba to carry on.

Watching that movie as an adult and a father, I couldn't help but to think about my very own legacy. Although I don't have a son (yet), I couldn't help but to think about what I will leave behind for my daughters. What I am doing today is bigger than me. What I am doing today is for the future generations to come in my bloodline.

I have witnessed my grandparents work the 40-50-40 lifestyle their whole life and have nothing to show for it but worn out bodies and social security checks. I've seen so many around me work their whole life, just to pay bills and die. I've seen poor generational habits and curses be passed down to the next generation. I have two daughters of my own now, so listen to me very closely when I say those poor generational habits and generational poverty are ending with me. I'm turning this ship into a new direction for the future of my family's legacy.

Maybe you only have a significant other right now. Maybe you have a significant other and children. Maybe you're single and don't have a significant other or have any children, but you hope someday to have that in your life. Maybe you don't want children (I would say maybe you don't want to get married, but that would be a lie because we all need/want love and affection at some point in life). Regardless of where you are currently, there is something you and I have in common; our lives are bigger than us.

There are two things that I knew I didn't want for my children: (1) I didn't want them to grow up fatherless just as I did, because I knew the effect of a father not being active in his child's life; (2) and I didn't want my children growing up in the environments I had to grow up in.

Thanks to Jay-Z's album *4:44* with a song called "Legacy" on it (as well as all the gems he has put in his older music) and *The Lion King*, I really started planning for the future. I really started playing the long game. Chess became more than a board game for me; it became life. I really started carefully calculating every move that I made, and before each move, I will ask myself if it's going to set my family up or set my family back.

Are You Setting Up Or Setting Back?

If you are a parent or plan on having a family in the future, ask yourself if you are setting the future generations up, or if are you are setting the future generations back with the decisions you are making today. If you don't take anything else away from this book, please take away the fact you are NOT the only one who's impacted by YOUR choices. Your family is directly impacted by the decisions you make. Let's look at two examples.

Let's say a guy whose name is Mr. Wasted grew up in poverty, and at the age of 26, has become a father. He grew up without much, so now he goes shopping all of the time for designer clothing and is always the first one in line for Jordans when they release. He buys all the jewelry and keeps a nice car as well.

His friends want him to party and "turn up" every weekend, so he goes out spending big money while smoking a ton of weed and drinking all of the liquor that he can. He gets so wasted and sometimes does not know how he makes it back home. He appears to be "living the life" right now.

So far, through his actions and decisions, is he setting his children up for success, or is he setting his children back? What can his children learn and apply from him that will help them in life? Let's continue.

Twenty years have passed, and Mr. Wasted is now 46 still living the same life that he was living twenty years ago. He's still buying all of the clothes, shoes, jewelry, and cars. He has bought all the toys and spends big every year on Christmas for his kids. He can't seem to keep a decent woman, so he's unmarried. He still gets drunk, high, and tries to keep up with the parties.

One night after another *wasted* party, he didn't make it back home. He actually got shot at the party by accident and died on the scene. Mr. Wasted didn't have any money saved up before he died. Now his family has to scrape money together for his funeral costs or start a GoFundMe campaign to raise money. Most importantly, his children are left behind with nothing because he didn't own any assets and he did not have a life insurance policy in place before he passed away.

The life insurance policy at the very least could have paid for his children's future college expenses, or helped his family be in a good financial position after his passing. As a result of his actions and decisions in life, he didn't set his kids up. Instead, he set them back. He set his family back at least another generation.

On the flip side, let's say you have Mr. Ambition who is 26 and also has children. He shops occasionally from time to time, but when he does, he tries to search for bargain deals. He pays cash for affordable cars. He may grab a drink occasionally, but he doesn't party heavily. He has goals of starting his own business in the near future so that he can start working towards building financial freedom for himself and his family.

Twenty years later, Mr. Wealthy is now 46. Because Mr. Wealthy didn't choose to live a wild adult life, he was able to make much more progress than Mr. Wasted. He got connected with a financial advisor back in his 20s who advised him to take out a life insurance policy so that his family can be good financially, just in case something were to happen to him while he's working towards his goal of financial freedom.

He also had permanent life insurance policies on his children which he was also able to build cash value inside the policy. He was able to pay for his children's college expenses out of pocket by taking out the cash value that had accumulated in the life insurance policy.

In addition to the life insurance policies, he spent the last twenty years building his real estate investment company and has built that into a multi-million dollar company. So not only would he be leaving money behind with his life insurance, he has a multi-million dollar business and assets that he can pass down to his children and family as well. As a result of the decisions and actions in his life, he was able to live a good healthy life, set his children up for success, and teach them how to keep their family legacy growing in the right direction.

Now, based off those two examples, you can tell which one had the better lifestyle to model after. You're also probably thinking that I'm saying that you can't have "any fun" or that you have to be serious and uptight with your life the whole time in order to build a good life for you and your family. That's not what I'm saying at all. I encourage you to have fun in your life. In fact, you *need* fun in your life. I'm just saying you have to be wise with your decisions, especially if you have children and a family. You have to think with the mentality of setting your children and future generations up for success.

Let me be clear, setting your children up doesn't just mean financially. Setting up your children also means creating a positive loving environment inside the home as well as placing them in a good environment outside of the home. What is the energy like in your household? What do your children see when they step outside of your home? Do they see drug dealing, hear gun shots, witness fights, and or see drunks hanging out in front of the ABC store? Or do they see nice beautiful homes, individuals with nice paying jobs, and nice businesses in the area? What words are you speaking into their life? Does your child always hear you tell them that they are "bad," or are you speaking positive words of affirmation into their life every day?

Education starts at home first and foremost. You must allow them to make mistakes, but be there to coach them through their mishaps. Yelling and whipping them isn't going to make them totally understand. You must be able to teach them at any moment. Teaching doesn't just start when your child goes to school.

Teaching starts the moment they enter this world. Ages 0-5 are their grooming years. They are sponges. They are learning everything, good and bad, that you show and teach them. Teach them things that you wish you would have known at their age. Instill them with knowledge that will help them win in life.

The Marathon Continues...Legacy

"Open trust accounts and deposit racks, million-dollar life

insurance on my flesh."- Nipsey Hussle

First and foremost, I want to take a moment to salute, and say Rest In Power to investor, business mogul, and Hip Hop artist Nipsey Hussle. What he did for his family and for my culture in the short time that he was here on earth was impeccable. If you let critics tell it, they would just call him another Crip gangbanger from the slums of Los Angeles, California. I'm about to give you a little background of Nipsey Hussle if you don't know who he is by now, and how he relates to this chapter.

Although Nipsey Hussle, whose real name is Ermias Ashedom, is known to the world as a rapper, those of us who have been following him knows that, like Jay-Z, he was more than just a rapper. He was a savvy businessman.

Nipsey owned a clothing line/store with his FAMILY called

The Marathon Clothing that is located inside of a plaza; the very same plaza in which he grew up right down the street from; the very same plaza/corner where he hustled at in his younger days. That is the very same plaza that he and his real estate investment partner, Dave Gross, bought for a couple million.

Nipsey died at the age 33, but he was way ahead of the game when it came to setting up his children, his family, his community, and his legacy. Although he may have enjoyed the finer things in life such as Benzes, Bentleys, and private jets, he was still thinking about things that most people don't think about until later in life, or never think about at all. He said he opened trust funds and deposited "racks" for his children. He said he put a million-dollar life insurance policy on *his flesh.*

In just 33 short years (and really shorter time than that), Nipsey Hussle accomplished more than what the average person would even come close to accomplishing in a longer life span. He built wealth and a legacy that he passed along to his children and family. Nipsey put all the chips on himself and made investments into the music business, clothing business, real estate investments, a partnership with Puma, and other business endeavors before his death.

Nipsey was preparing his family for a marathon, not a 100-meter sprint. Hence to why he named his clothing brand The Marathon Clothing. Everything that he did was not only for his benefit, but for the benefit of his family. After his death, millions of people supported The Marathon Clothing brand (which his family still owns and runs) even more, and the brand has made an upward of $10 million plus in merchandise sales.

His family is still benefiting from the revenue that's being generated from his music catalog. His children have trust funds in place that he set up, and he left a million dollars for them from a life insurance he put in place.

He brought change to his local community on Slauson Avenue in Los Angeles. He was a Crip gang member, but he brought unity amongst rival gangs. He left wealth, knowledge, and lessons for his children and family to carry out over future generations. He inspired millions of people like me to work on preparing our families for the marathon. His legacy will never be forgotten; at least not with me. The marathon continues!

So What Are You Going To Do About Your Marathon?

There's not many of us who take planning for our death and legacy as serious as we should. A lot of people have died without a will in place. There is no escaping death. It's a part of life. It's not a matter of if you are going to die, but a matter of when you are going to die. The question is: how are you preparing your family for your departure someday?

I read the book, *Notes From The Wake Up Call: Financial Inspiration Learned From 4:44* written by "The Financial Motivator" Ash Cash Exantus. In the book, he breaks down financial lessons from Jay-Z's album *4:44*. He says, "70% of wealthy families lose their wealth by the second generation, and 90% by the third." Once again, whether you have children, plan on having children, or don't want any at all; you should definitely take your legacy serious.

Let's wrap this chapter up by talking about what you and I can do about our legacies.

First and foremost, we must educate ourselves. I can't stress the importance of education enough, and I'm not just talking about college. I'm talking about things that college *don't* teach you. I'm talking about becoming financially literate. We can't afford to still keep the same old habits. We must get smarter and better with our finances. We must learn how to create financial game plans. We must learn how to go from earned income to creating passive income as I discussed in chapter 6. We must learn different strategies to build wealth.

We must learn the difference between assets and liabilities. We must understand interest rates when negotiating deals on houses, cars, and loans. We must learn about retirement accounts. We must learn about insurance policies. We must learn wills and trust funds. I can go on and on, but the point is this: in order to begin building a legacy, we must unlearn some bad habits and learn new habits and better knowledge that can help us win. We must learn the financial lingo and knowledge first before we can play the wealth building game, if in fact we want to pass down generational wealth.

"Why is it important to educate myself first, Jared?" I'm glad you asked. It is important for you to educate yourself because you must be able to teach your children and family the knowledge, so that they will know how to maintain the legacy that you build. They must be taught about what it took to create it and understand the work that is required to keep it alive and prosperous.

"I don't know anybody who can teach me, so how can I learn?" One way you can learn is by turning the TV off, getting off of Facebook, Snapchat, and Instagram, and picking up a book. Nipsey Hussle said that he was a "book junkie." In fact, most of the wealthy are "book junkies."

I read in a CNBC article once that the average worker reads an average of less than one book a year and works an average of 37.5 hours a week. This same person makes 319 times less money than the top U.S. CEOs who claim to read more than 60 books a year. Just ask Bill Gates who once said that he reads about 60 books a year.

Study the wealthy. Study their actions from the past that have gotten them (and their families) where they are today. Read books that many of them have written. Watch/listen to the knowledge they put out in their interviews and speaking engagements. The knowledge is out there, but YOU have to go and get it for yourself.

Having a good financial advisor on your team is also a major plus. Getting a financial advisor was one of the best choices I have made in my young life. My financial advisor has helped with financial planning for my family, helped me find "lost money" by seeing what areas I can cut back on expenses, and holds me accountable for making sure I put my family in the best possible position.

Conclusion

"Generational wealth, that's the key/ My parents ain't have sh*t, so that ship started with me"- Jay-Z

Remember, just because you were born in the struggle doesn't mean you have to stay in the struggle. That doesn't mean your children have to struggle. The goal is to elevate in life and become the trailblazer for your family. We have to stop living like it's normal to struggle. Going broke for your kids, but not building wealth for your kids should not be ok.

There is no wealth potential in just working a job. It is the owner who will benefit long term from a worker's long hours. While the wealthy are passing businesses and assets down to their children and family, we are leaving our children and family with bills and expenses. It's time that we change that narrative. It's time that we stop looking at wealth as a luxury, and more of a necessity. It's time that we take our legacy more serious.

Let's stop using "you can't take money with you when you die" as an excuse to remain broke and throw our hard-earned dollars away. You're not supposed to take it with you. You're supposed to build assets and create wealth that can be passed down.

How do you think the wealthy families remain wealthy over time? Someone in the family stepped up and educated his or herself and passed their knowledge to their children along with assets. We give our children video games, phones, and tablets. Meanwhile, the wealthy are giving their children business and financial lessons, books to read, and traveling with them around the world.

Let's stop making our families suffer from our poor financial choices. We have to stop giving our children ultimatums or forcing them out of the house at 18. Parenting doesn't stop after high school. You are aiding the financial chaos when you tell your child to fend for themselves out here in this world if you haven't prepared them.

Teach them about bills and credit. Make them contribute to the household instead of telling them to build on what you can barely do yourself. Give them your shoulders to stand on. That's what generational wealth is. It's about them picking up where you left off; not leaving them worst off.

If you are older and reading this, think back to when you were 18 or even a young adult. Do you feel like you were prepared to survive in this world, or do you wish you could have stayed home a little while longer? Do you wish your parents didn't force you to go to "college"? Do you wish they didn't force you out of the house? Well, you can't go back and change that, but you can equip your children (or future children) with the knowledge and tools for them to win in their lives and carry on anything you're trying to build.

If you are young and reading this, don't allow society to make you feel bad for living at home with your parents. If your parents give you the opportunity to live there for as long as you need to then take it, but don't abuse it. Don't just live there and be reluctant to what your parents are trying to teach you. Soak up as much knowledge as you can from your parents as they try to prepare you for life.

Just like Mufasa, Nipsey Hussle, and Jay-Z, I'm building to pass down a legacy to my children. Yes, it's a much harder road than just settling for another company's $30 hour job, but I can't pass that company down to my children! I'm not doing this just to get rich. I'm doing this to place my daughter and future generations that will come behind me in a better position.

My parents, and my wife's parents, did the best that they could with what they had to work with, but now it's up to us to take it to another level and start our children off ahead, rather than behind. I hustle the way I do because I have two daughters and a wife who look to me for safety and security. I don't ever want them to ask me for something and I have to say, "I don't have it." Creating a family that stays a family is one of my biggest goals in life.

Therefore, I'll continue to make key investments, take risks, bear the most pressure, always remain a lifelong student, and allow my daughters to stay at home for as long as they need to. I'm not pushing them out of the house at 18. I have life insurance policies and trust funds in place for my ladies. I plan on leaving businesses and real estate for my family as well. This ship started with me.

Chapter 10

Success Is My Prey

"I don't want to make it look easy; I want to make it look

possible!"

What does success mean? Well, it could mean a lot of things depending on one's perspective. The good news is that it's not a right or wrong answer to that question. Success to me may mean something totally different to you. Regardless of what the formal definition is, *success is your prey* and *success is my prey,* and we are about to discuss what I mean by that, as this is the reason that I wrote this book.

To achieve success in any area of your life, you must first refuse to settle for anything average in your life. Throw away average thinking, average goals, average money, average living, average jobs, etc. When the *average* individual says, "The sky is the limit," I say that's average/limited thinking. Don't tell me the sky is the limit when there are claims that Neil Armstrong put his footprints on the moon in 1969.

When I say *success is my prey,* I am talking about being aggressively ambitious and relentless towards achieving my goals in life. It means that I set goals and don't stop until those goals are met. It means that I won't let anything get in the way of my prey. It means not being afraid to take risks. It means that every time I bet on me, I win. It means aiming for perfection but falling on excellence.

Every time I hit a goal, I set another. I'd rather have lots of small successes than hope for a big one. A lot can happen to discourage you if you' waiting on a goal that's too high to hit within a reasonable time frame.

I've always had the underdog mentality growing up. That mentality has gotten me to where I am today. I've never liked the easy way out or asked for any handouts. My mom instilled that in me as a young boy. Whenever older people randomly gave my siblings and me some money, my mom made us give it right back to those individuals. Mama said, "Don't ever accept handouts in life, because things in life aren't free. If you want it, then go get it." So, everything that I have in my life thus far, has been brought to me by my impeccable work ethic, thanks to Mama.

But it's not enough to just work hard to get it. You got to work twice as hard to maintain and elevate your success even more. I'm talking about playing like you're in first but working like you're in second. I'm talking about remaining humble when you achieve success but hungry enough to get more and take it to another level.

People like Tom Brady show us a beautiful example of what it looks like to be humble but hungry. He continues to get better each year. He has won quite a few rings, but he starts each season as if he's still chasing his first one.

The way he grinds and works to perfect his craft is what makes him different. The way he studies teams and can pick a defense apart is what makes him different. His drive to still win as a 42-year-old quarterback, and his strive to be number one after of all these years is what makes him different. He has tortured every team that passed up on him in the 2000 NFL draft. *Success is his prey,* and he still plays with the same underdog spirit that he had when he got drafted in the 6th round.

He didn't just work hard to obtain success and quit. He has worked just as hard to maintain success by remaining humble but hungry, and that is what makes him the GOAT! Getting better and never settling is what drives me also!

When I got my first job, I was working at a warehouse making minimum wage at $7.25 an hour. The best company in the area was BMW, so I made BMW my target (prey). Each job that I took after leaving my first warehouse job was strengthening my resume. I was strategically taking jobs that would make me more valuable in my industry. That even included going to BMW through a temp agency the first time. However, in order for me to land a full-time position at BMW, I had to leave the company.

I had to leave the temp agency because BMW wasn't hiring for my position at the time, so I was basically stuck. However, an opportunity presented itself and this lion was in position to strike. BMW had done something that was almost unheard of, and that was, hiring directly from outside of the company. Normally, the only way someone could get hired was by working through the temp agency that had the direct contract with BMW.

When I heard the news of the company doing direct hiring from the outside, I found another job, put in my notice, and left the temp agency. I left with one goal in mind: come back to BMW as a direct hire. I applied for a direct hire position with BMW and passed all of the requirements.

After passing all of the requirements, then the hardest part came; the waiting period. I was waiting so long for them to call me back that I actually had gotten discouraged. After a year and a half of waiting and working some crappy jobs (I say crappy because the labor wasn't too pleasing), I finally got the call that I had been waiting for. Not only did I come back to BMW directly hired on, but I got in the department that I wanted when I was out there the first time as a temp.

Yes, I worked hard and had to patiently wait until I finally got that prey, but I still had to show up daily in order for me to have achieved that goal. One thing that I want you remember on your success journey is that you MUST show up daily. Your biggest achievements are found in your daily actions. Tom Brady didn't just randomly win super bowls. He won super bowls because he showed up to practice daily, he studied film even after practices, he worked on his game in the "off season," and he showed up to win games. Spectators just see the end results of success; they don't see the actions that the players and team put in daily to achieve such high success.

Before I came back to BMW, I had to show up daily at those crappy jobs. I had to maintain great attendance, great job performance, and no disciplinary actions. I had to build a solid resume. I don't just wait for an interview to get ready. I'm always prepared for an interview by the way I dress daily, the way I speak, and the way I interact with others. I'm always working on my interview skills. I'm always working on any skills that would increase my chances of hitting my big targets.

So again, set big goals (prey) in your life, but also set smaller goals that you can hit daily. This doesn't just apply to sports or careers. This applies to any area of your life. Ask yourself this question, "What can I do or learn today that will help me reach my future goals/prey?"

Face it...Chase it!

Yes, I've witnessed both of my parents go to prison, but I'm also blessed to have both of my parents here today in good health and better positions. I've also been a convicted felon myself, but now I'm a husband, father, and a leader. I've witnessed shootouts and drug dealing, but I've also witnessed living in peaceful communities/environments. I've witnessed seeing family members that I love get hooked on hard drugs, but now I see those very same people being naturally high off life because of their success.

I've experienced eating out of QuikTrip trash cans late at night, but I've also enjoyed good dinner and good views at the Sun Dial restaurant at the top of the "W" in Atlanta. I graduated with a GED, and I've experienced working minimum wage, but I've also experienced what ownership in a business can do as well. I've slept on the couch, I've slept on the floor, I've slept in a shelter, but I've never slept on myself.

I'm not saying all of this again to "rub it in" or anything. I'm saying this as another reminder that life at times won't be easy, but getting to a better life is totally possible! I'm saying this again to remind you of just how far I've come because I declared to make *success my prey*.

People ask me how I go so hard on my grind, and I reply, "How could I not, coming from where I come from?" Hustling and grinding has become a lifestyle for me. This isn't anything that I just turn off and on. This is something that stays on, because if not, then I'll be right back where I started.

I knew that if I wanted to build a future that is better than my past, then I would have to declare it. I felt like I owed it to myself to be great and not settle for average or mediocre. It was up to me to go get my *prey*; not anyone else. I had to take control of destiny. I refused to accept the environment that I was born into. I wanted to experience another side of life, and when I became an adult, I went after everything I wanted.

After watching *CSI: Miami* and the *Bad Boys* movies, and gazing at how beautiful Miami was on TV, I made Miami my *prey*, so the first time I stepped on a plane, I was headed to Miami. I actually went twice in the same year! Since I've experienced living around drugs and in bug-infested cheap motels, I like to enjoy top floor suites and nice resorts now. Since I didn't have much growing up, I now enjoy the finer things that life has to offer.

As I got older, I stopped being envious of people who had more wealth or were in better positions than me and started learning from those people because I realized they weren't any different than me. They just declared what they wanted and went after it. While I may have started off with the odds stacked against me, I still had the same opportunity as them to declare and create the life that I wanted. It was simply up to me to get it.

Just as it was up to me to declare and create the life that I wanted, it is up to you also. You owe it to yourself to be great. You don't have to settle for where you are currently at in life. Regardless of what people are telling you, what the statistics say, or who doesn't support you, you can declare and take action for more success in your life. Believe in yourself and have supreme confidence in your ability to win. Bet on yourself every time. When they tell you that you can't do something, that is just a reflection of their limitation, not yours.

People don't believe in you and support you? So what, just be sure that you believe in you and support your own self. You must take control of your life and own your destiny. You want to start that business? Declare it and go get it. You want better health? Declare it and go get it. You want that job with great pay and benefits? Declare it and go get it. You want a great marriage? Declare it and go get it. You want that million dollars by 30? Declare it, and by all means neccessary, go get it!

You must declare and manifest any success that you want in your life. I'm a walking witness that good things come to those that get off their butt and work for it. Everything that I have today I spoke it into existence. Privilege didn't get me to where I'm at today. My work ethic got me here.

I created a *success is my prey* declaration that I read to myself every morning and every night, and I want to share it with you. You can use mine or create your own, but I want you to practice declaring and affirming what you want in your life.

Success Is My Prey Declaration

I, _____ , declare that *Success Is My Prey*. I will do everything in my ability to create a better life for myself. Everything I do is successful, and I can do anything I set my mind to achieve. I have no fear of anything, and I do everything well. I will not allow my past to hold me back, and I will use it as motivation. I will no longer have a poor relationship with my finances. I will take my credit serious. I will seek to build wealth and pass along a legacy that I can be proud of. I will continue being a lifelong student, and pass along any knowledge that I learn with my family and peers around me. I will always win in life, because even when I lose, I still win. I understand that a loss is really a valuable lesson. I declare that *success is my prey* and I will continue to elevate in life!

Signature_____Date_____

Last Word

You did it! You have completed this book! I hope that you have found this book to be very useful for your journey in life. I have been elevating myself with what I have shared in this book, so I felt compelled to share my story and these lessons with you. I felt that there was someone else that I could help with this book. I hope that someone is you. Even if you only take one chapter, one paragraph, or one sentence and applied it to your life, I have done my job. I want to see you win just as much as I win. After all, we ALL can win in this lifetime. There's enough success to go around for everybody. I wish you much success on your journey. Now go and get your PREY!

Thanks for reading! If you enjoyed this book or found it useful I'd be very grateful if you'd post a short review on Amazon or send feedback on my social media. Your support really does make a difference and I read all the reviews personally so I can get your feedback and make this book as well as my future books even better.

Thanks again for your support!

ACKNOWLEDGEMENTS

First, I would like to thank my wife for always believing in me, encouraging me, and standing by my side. We have endured a lot over the years. I couldn't ask for a better life partner, business partner, and mother of my children. Without my queen, I can only go so far, but with my queen, there is no limit as to how far I can go. So, I thank her for helping me become a better man and husband daily. I would like to thank my children for continuing to help me become a better man and father daily as well.

Secondly, I would like to thank my mother and father for supporting me on my first book project, my business ventures, and just life in general. I am their firstborn, so my mission is to make them proud as much as I can here on earth. I would also like to thank my grandparents, my aunts, my uncles, and my cousins on both sides of my family, as well as my wife's family.

There's a long list, so I don't want to risk missing anyone, but I would like to thank all of my close friends for their die- hard love and support. I thank these gentlemen for their support and for keeping me encouraged to grow as a husband, father, leader, entrepreneur, and a man. Those guys totally rock.

I would like to thank everyone locally, as well as those around the world for their support. I am thankful for the love that I received for my business ventures, and I seek to always give back and return it 10 times greater.

Finally, I would like to thank you, the reader, for reading and supporting my first of many books. I hope that I have been and continue to be a great help to you on your journey!

I love you all!

About The Author

 Jared "J.ANDERS" Smith is one of the nation's top rising motivators and coaches on success, finances, and relationships. He is a published author, motivational speaker, investor, and entrepreneur. Dubbed as the "voice of the underdog" he shares his bold positivity and high energy to really connect with people.

Although he's only in his 20s, Jared has made it his mission to help people maximize their full potential by giving them the tools, resources, and inspiration needed from his debut book *Success Is My Prey*.

Jared has been inspiring and motivating others long before becoming an author or speaking in front of large audiences. His first opportunity to speak and empower others came when he was a 17 year old inmate in Gwinnett County jail facing 20 years of prison. From that point forward he vowed to elevate his life, make success his prey, and help others in the process.

Today, he uses personal stories from his own life journey to provide insight to others about how to accomplish their prey. He aims to travel the country and provide individuals and businesses with the tools needed to redefine their mind and environments, so they can create the space necessary for the important positive shifts that make every day better than the last. With exceptional guidance and contagious enthusiasm and entertainment, Jared guarantees a lasting impression anywhere he goes.

He is a husband and a father of two beautiful girls. He enjoys spending time with family and friends. When he's not writing, speaking, coaching others, or working on business, Jared enjoys traveling, play golf, playing basketball, reading, playing chess, and doing volunteer work.

Jared would like to hear from you! So here's how you can connect with him. You can email him personally at jared@jandersinspires.com. Also, be sure to follow him on social media.

FACEBOOK: search Jared "J.ANDERS" Smith.

INSTAGRAM: @j.andersinspires

SNAPCHAT: @Rockcooley

Visit jandersinspires.com to receive updates about new book releases and speaking engagements.

Made in the USA
Columbia, SC
16 June 2020